Establishing a Lasting Legacy

Six Steps to Maximize Your Leadership Impact
and Improve Teacher Retention

BECKY EVERS-GERDES   RYAN SIEGLE

Solution Tree | Press

a division of
Solution Tree

555 North Morton Street
Bloomington, IN 47404
800.733.6786 (toll free) / 812.336.7700
FAX: 812.336.7790

email: info@SolutionTree.com
SolutionTree.com

Visit **go.SolutionTree.com/leadership** to download the free reproducibles in this book.

Printed in the United States of America

Library of Congress Cataloging-in-Publication Data

Names: Evers-Gerdes, Becky, author. | Siegle, Ryan, author.
Title: Establishing a lasting legacy : six steps to maximize your
   leadership impact and improve teacher retention / Becky Evers-Gerdes,
   Ryan Siegle.
Description: Bloomington : Solution Tree Press, 2021. | Includes
   bibliographical references and index.
Identifiers: LCCN 2021035544 (print) | LCCN 2021035545 (ebook) | ISBN
   9781952812156 (paperback) | ISBN 9781952812163 (ebook)
Subjects: LCSH: Teacher turnover--Prevention. | Educational leadership. |
   Teacher-principal relationships. | School environment.
Classification: LCC LB2840.2 .E94 2021 (print) | LCC LB2840.2 (ebook) |
   DDC 371.14--dc23
LC record available at https://lccn.loc.gov/2021035544
LC ebook record available at https://lccn.loc.gov/2021035545

Solution Tree
Jeffrey C. Jones, CEO
Edmund M. Ackerman, President

Solution Tree Press
President and Publisher: Douglas M. Rife
Associate Publisher: Sarah Payne-Mills
Art Director: Rian Anderson
Managing Production Editor: Kendra Slayton
Copy Chief: Jessi Finn
Production Editor: Alissa Voss
Content Development Specialist: Amy Rubenstein
Copy Editor: Kate St. Ives
Proofreader: Elisabeth Abrams
Text and Cover Designer: Laura Cox
Editorial Assistants: Sarah Ludwig and Elijah Oates

For my mother and father, Norbert and Carol Evers, who first taught me the importance of faith, family, and shining your light brightly for others to see; and to my husband, Scott, and especially my children, Nathan, Matthew, and Grace, who continue to be my best reasons for doing so.

—Becky Evers-Gerdes

To my children, Owen and Elin, may you always realize the incredible, positive impact of your influence on others. Strive to make good choices, work hard, and be kind. I'm so proud of you!

To my wife, Kirsten, thank you for walking side by side with me through this journey. You are selfless and loyal, and you have helped me become a better person.

To the servant leaders that have paved the way for me, including my parents and grandparents, thank you for modeling what it means to establish a legacy where people come first.

—Ryan Siegle

Acknowledgments

With appreciation and respect for our colleagues: Cheri R. Herbst, Cynthia A. Wiest, Scott Dart, Dr. Wayne Samson, Sean Martinson, the family of Dr. Ed Richardson, Ryan DeBay, the ISD 318 fifth-grade family, Dean Jennissen, Dr. Valerie Aimakhu, Derek Brown, Dr. Ruben Rivera, Dee Sabol, Crystal Hintzman, Jamie Wiech, Norma Olson, Rich Schoenert, Linda Schmidt, Dr. Julie Carlson, Dr. Fatima Lawson, Melissa Uetz, and our friends and colleagues at Bethel University. Thank you for your partnership, dedication to quality, and capacity to bring insight and joy to our shared work. A special thank you to Solution Tree for providing us a platform to share our voice.

—Becky Evers-Gerdes and Ryan Siegle

Solution Tree Press would like to thank the following reviewers:

Kyley Cumbow
Principal
Georgia Morse Middle School
Pierre, South Dakota

Cassandra Erkens
Consultant and Author
Lakeville, Minnesota

Clay Gleason
Principal
Hollis Elementary School
Hollis, Maine

Chris Hansen
Director of Learning
Hortonville Area School District
Hortonville, Wisconsin

Shavon Jackson
Principal
Crawford Elementary School
Russellville, Arkansas

Lance McClard
Principal
North Elementary School
Jackson, Missouri

Kecia Ray
Educational Consultant
K20Connect
Nashville, Tennessee

Luke Spielman
Principal
Park View Middle School
Mukwonago, Wisconsin

Dianne Yee
Superintendent, School Improvement
Calgary Board of Education
Calgary, Alberta, Canada

Visit **go.SolutionTree.com/leadership** to download the free reproducibles in this book.

Table of Contents

Reproducible pages are in italics.

About the Authors

 **Becky Evers-Gerdes, EdD,** is the dean of academics at Loyola Catholic School in Mankato, Minnesota. Her experiences include serving as an educator and administrator at the elementary, middle, and high school levels, including in schools designated as needing to make an improvement by the Minnesota Department of Education. Becky's additional titles include K–12 curriculum director, staff development coordinator, special education coordinator, and title program director. At the undergraduate and graduate levels, Becky has served as a course developer and designer for Bethel University and as an adjunct faculty member for Minnesota State University, Bethel University, and Concordia University in the areas of leadership, research, and K–12 education and special education. Using ongoing student data and culturally responsive teaching, she focuses on social-emotional learning being as equally important as academics and strong parent and community partnerships.

Becky credits the great educators she has worked with for receiving the following awards: Southwest Minnesota State University Leadership Award, Celebration School Recognition (expertly documenting efforts to increase student achievement), Reward School Recognition (highest performing fifteen percent of Title I schools in the state), Feinstein's Good Deeds School Recognition, Environmental Awareness Award, Emerging Minnesota Schools of Character Award, and Academic Excellence Foundation (MAEF) School Spotlight Award.

Becky has led teams and departments through unpacking standards, aligning standards to coursework, and ensuring that formative and summative assessments are analyzed. Becky has also been active in co-presenting teacher retention solutions to professional organizations and independent school districts.

Becky earned her doctoral degree in education administration from Bethel University and holds a specialist and master of education administration degree from Minnesota State University, Mankato, along with a bachelor of science degree in elementary education from Southwest Minnesota State University, Marshall.

Ryan Siegle, EdD, currently serves as a classroom teacher for Independent School District 318 in Grand Rapids, Minnesota. He is passionate about transforming school and classroom cultures and believes in the need for supporting both the whole child and the whole teacher. His focus areas of research include leadership factors influencing the retention of teachers, servant leadership, trust, school culture, and school climate.

Ryan has been highly involved in teacher retention and mentorship at the school, district, and state levels. He has experience working with both teachers and educational leaders on the topic of teacher retention, support, and building teacher self-efficacy. Ryan has most recently provided formal presentations and training for school districts and professional organizations examining the impact of teacher turnover and how leaders can address this issue within their schools. He has also helped influence state-level policy decisions, focusing specifically on best practice teaching induction and mentoring.

Ryan holds a doctoral degree in education administration from Bethel University in St. Paul, Minnesota. He has also earned a master's of curriculum and instruction from St. Catherine University in St. Paul, Minnesota, and a bachelor of arts degree in elementary education from Concordia College in Moorhead, Minnesota.

To book Becky Evers-Gerdes or Ryan Siegle for professional development, contact pd@SolutionTree.com.

Introduction
What Will Be Your Legacy?

Are you on this planet to do something, or are
you here just for something to do? If you're on
this planet to do something, then what is it?
What difference will you make? What will be
your legacy?

—James M. Kouzes and Barry Posner

The new school gymnasium was packed for the event. The pep band blared music, a buzz of laughter and conversation filled the air, and the crowd eagerly anticipated the start of the evening. Have you ever been to an event like this—immersed in an atmosphere so palpable you could almost feel it? *This* was one of those nights. This was a night many had waited for. A night to celebrate and to honor an individual who had made a difference in all of their lives.

Trying to fully comprehend how one man could have such a monumental impact on an individual, a school, and a community, Ryan stood watching, staring at the crowd. It was a crowd that filled the stands from the basketball floor to the top of the bleachers. A crowd of people coming from near and far. A crowd of rich and poor. A crowd of young and old. A crowd with one common thread—a teacher, their leader, who had made each and every one of them feel like they were the most important person in the world.

In the minutes to come, members from that crowd would walk down, one by one, and share their stories, celebrating their long-time leader and the contribution he made to the school community he had served. They would speak of his leadership, selflessness, and service, and how he was authentic to the core. They would mention his character and his ability to see potential in others even when they didn't see it in themselves. They would remark on his uncanny aptitude to unite a group of individuals under one common purpose. But, most importantly, they would reflect on his legacy and how it was ingrained in the culture and character of the school and community. It was because of this legacy that the school community was proud to unveil the name of the building that night—*his name,* Ryan's grandfather's name, set to adorn the side of the building for generations to come.

There are certain leaders we as educators come across in life who have a unique ability to empower us to become the best version of ourselves. These leaders find a way to meet us at our own level, guiding us to believe in ourselves, supporting our unique path and purpose, and helping us to discover the innate value in others. Eventually, these leaders transcend time and leave the kind of legacy that packs the house in a gymnasium, influences the naming of a building, or is ingrained in the culture of a school.

We define a school leader's legacy as:

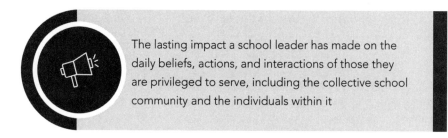

The lasting impact a school leader has made on the daily beliefs, actions, and interactions of those they are privileged to serve, including the collective school community and the individuals within it

Have you ever wondered how one person can leave such a legacy—one that positively reaches the lives of hundreds, if not thousands of people? Have you considered your legacy and what *you* will leave behind? Your legacy will not come from your achievements, title, or positional power, or from how you climbed the professional ladder. Your legacy does not hinge on your success with student achievement numbers, attendance records, or graduation rates. Instead, *your legacy remains within and through the people that you serve long after you're gone.* But, if people don't *remain,* it doesn't matter what you do. Your legacy depends on the collective group existing and sustaining within that community. In large part, your legacy is dependent on the issue of teacher retention.

A Teacher Retention Problem

Each year new teachers enter the teaching profession with a sense of eagerness and anticipation with the hope of making a difference and changing the world. Yet, within a few short years, many of these same teachers leave the profession disillusioned and disheartened, ultimately packing their bags in search of a new career where they feel valued and find success. Approximately eight percent of teachers choose to leave teaching every year (Carver-Thomas & Darling-Hammond, 2017). Beginning teachers leave at an even more rampant pace, with up to 30 percent of teachers leaving the profession within the first five years (Sutcher, Darling-Hammond, & Carver-Thomas, 2016). This is a problem for national teacher shortages considering attrition rates make up almost 90 percent of annual teacher demand (Carver-Thomas & Darling-Hammond, 2017). However, attrition rates alone do not reveal the magnitude of problems left behind from teachers leaving their positions.

Annually, 16 percent of all teachers either quit the profession or leave their school in search of another school to work (Carver-Thomas & Darling-Hammond, 2017). The Alliance for Excellent Education suggests the cost of teacher attrition in the United States can be as high as $2.2 billion per year (Haynes, 2014). For you, a school leader, that means when people leave your building, you then need to spend additional time and money on recruiting, hiring, orienting, and training new staff. Your professional development offerings need to increase so new staff can get up to speed. Your student achievement, staff morale, collegiality, and collaboration decrease as it takes time for new teachers to settle into the demands and responsibilities of their new jobs. The list of roadblocks goes on and on and on.

There is no denying the teaching profession can be difficult on the mental health and well-being of teachers. Research suggests that teachers are feeling more overworked, stressed, and dissatisfied with their jobs than ever before (Shernoff, Mehta, Atkins, Torf, & Spencer, 2011). Several studies highlight the severity of the problems facing the teaching profession. The Learning Policy Institute reports 55 percent of teachers cited job dissatisfaction as a reason they chose to quit teaching (Sutcher et al., 2016). The report goes on to explain the impact dissatisfaction has on staff turnover by stating, "Most teachers who voluntarily leave the classroom list some area of job dissatisfaction as very important or extremely important in their decision to leave the profession" (Sutcher et al., 2016). When compared to other professions, teachers often have higher stress and more difficulty finding a balance between their personal lives and professional lives (Worth & Van den Brande, 2019). Another study found teachers consider their jobs stressful during almost two-thirds of the time they work, which is almost twice as high as those working outside of education (American Federation of Teachers, 2017). It's no wonder two-thirds of teachers that leave the profession do so before retirement (Carver-Thomas & Darling-Hammond, 2017). Figure I.1 (page 4) reflects additional research findings on common turnover factors.

There is little doubt the demands of the teaching profession have been dramatically elevated through high-stakes accountability systems and an increasing number of students coming to school with social-emotional needs from adverse childhood experiences. Such experiences include "various forms of physical and emotional abuse,

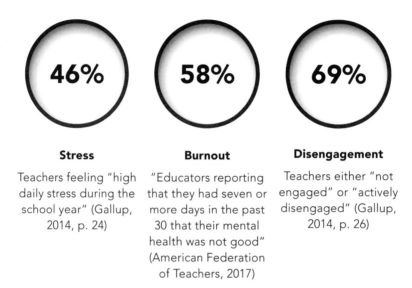

Stress

Teachers feeling "high daily stress during the school year" (Gallup, 2014, p. 24)

Burnout

"Educators reporting that they had seven or more days in the past 30 that their mental health was not good" (American Federation of Teachers, 2017)

Disengagement

Teachers either "not engaged" or "actively disengaged" (Gallup, 2014, p. 26)

Figure I.1: Findings related to teacher turnover.

neglect, and household dysfunction" (Center on the Developing Child, 2021). But cases such as these are vastly out of leaders' hands. So, what can you, as the leader of your school, do to retain your people? What factors within your influence are directly related to keeping your teachers in their classrooms and, in turn, helping them grow as educators?

Through our scholarly research, consulting with state-level organizations and independent school districts, and serving in several roles in both the K–12 and higher education settings, we've found several consistencies in why teachers leave the profession. Many of these consistencies point to the fact that a major influencer in teacher retention is the environment in which teachers work. Retention factors related to the school environment include leadership authenticity, collective and self-efficacy, trust, communication, and vision clarity, all of which we address throughout this book.

While there may not be a silver bullet to solving teacher retention concerns, the needle that weaves together the quilt of retention factors is *you*. No matter your teachers' ages, years of experience, or positions; no matter your school size, location, or grade orientation; the single most instrumental variable in elevating retention factors is the leader of the school (Hattie & Yates, 2014). As leaders, we can be at the front and center of responding to teacher turnover concerns by establishing a culture where people feel safe, valued, and cared for. When all is said and done, we have a responsibility to develop the working conditions necessary for the growth and sustainability of our teachers' professional needs (Liu & Hallinger, 2018; Tschannen-Moran & Gareis, 2015). Unfortunately, Leib Sutcher, Linda Darling-Hammond, and Desiree Carver-Thomas (2016) suggest "a lack of administrative support" (p. vi) is a primary reason that teachers leave their teaching positions. They go on to emphasize the vital role leaders play in the retention efforts of their teachers by stating:

> When teachers strongly disagree that their administrator encourages and acknowledges staff, communicates a clear vision, and generally runs a school well, turnover rates for movers and leavers jump to nearly one in four, more than double the rate of those who feel their administrators are supportive. (Sutcher et al., 2016, p. 51)

It is time that we as leaders understand the lynchpin of our leadership legacy is not about us at all. It's about the people *we keep* in our schools. Our legacy hinges on supporting our teachers and relating teacher retention to the reasons why teachers choose to teach in the first place. Educators go into the profession possessing a strong moral purpose for helping kids. Education is personal. Teaching is just as much about *who we are* as it is about what we teach. In other words, teaching is a "soul-craft," and teacher retention may be a matter of the heart (R. Rivera, personal communication, November 5, 2020). As the leader of your building, we strongly encourage you to consider what you are and are not doing to honor your lasting legacy and to bolster the retention of your teachers. We use the chapters of this book to help you do just that.

The Model

Living in Minnesota, we are quite familiar with the experience of standing alongside a lakeshore, grabbing a rock, and skipping it into the water. Like us, you've probably noticed when you throw that rock into the water, you essentially create a ripple effect—a system of concentric circles expanding from the very center of where that rock hit. Each ripple begins from the one before it and cannot fully form until the previous ripple has formed. Our Lasting Legacy model, shown in figure I.2 (page 6), follows a similar ripple pattern. Beginning in the center with "Who Am I?" and moving progressively outward, the development and maturation of each concept, in turn, set in motion the development and maturation of the next.

Lasting leadership must start from within the leader. When principals know who they are, teachers are more willing to trust them and engage in their work (Bird, Wang, Watson, & Murray, 2012). Principals with a strong understanding of themselves are more likely to influence the self-efficacy of their teachers (Feng, 2016) and, in turn, increase the retention factor of job satisfaction (Aldridge & Fraser, 2016). Therefore, the innermost ripple of our model asks the question, "Who am I?"

The second ripple asks the question, "Who are you?" When you discover who your teachers are as individuals, you can teach them to believe in themselves and look outside of themselves toward the greater school community (Shahidi, Shamsnia, & Baezat, 2015). The result is a wider legacy with beliefs and practices instilled within your teachers that will remain long after you are gone.

Figure I.2: Lasting Legacy model.

The third ripple asks the question, "Who are we?" After you have taken the time to know yourself (the first ripple) and your people (the second ripple), you are ready to work together toward collective teacher efficacy (the third ripple). Collective efficacy refers to your teachers' collective belief that they can accomplish things together. Your teachers' beliefs in each other will guide their actions and allow them to openly share, discuss, and collectively grow as a group.

The final question we ask is, "What matters most?" The answers to this question act as the final ripple, broadening your legacy through intentional practices to be applied at all points of your leadership journey. These high-leverage retention drivers are building and rebuilding trust, improving communication, and developing and casting a shared vision.

About the Book

This book walks you through the Lasting Legacy model so that you can implement it in your own school. In part one (chapters 1–3), we examine the *who* of your leadership legacy—Who Am I? Who Are You? Who Are We? Part two (chapters 4–6) examines What Matters Most?—the high-leverage drivers that will further widen your legacy and make teachers want to stay in your building.

In chapter 1, we discover how to know and grow *yourself* as an authentic leader. We will guide you through four dimensions of authenticity: (1) developing self-awareness, (2) embracing your core values, (3) practicing authentic decision making, and (4) increasing transparency with your staff.

Upon discovery of yourself, in chapter 2, we address how you can know and grow your *people* by elevating their sense of self-efficacy. We demonstrate how you can develop your teachers' self-efficacy by flipping the hierarchical model of leadership upside down and serving others by supporting them.

When a leader recognizes the individual strengths of their people, they must combine those individual strengths into a cohesive whole, where those strengths build on one another and reinforce our inherent need for each other. In chapter 3, we address how you can know and grow your *school* by developing collective efficacy. When collective efficacy is present, your school will become more than a place of work—it will become family. This chapter shows you how to help your teachers believe in their collective capabilities as they rely on interdependence and collaboration (Thiers, 2016).

A cohesive community experiences differing opinions, values, and perspectives. Chapter 4 focuses on how you can know and grow your *relationships* through building and rebuilding trust. You will accelerate your retention efforts and keep your teachers in your building when you examine your own trust-building behaviors, develop a positive narrative of trust in your school, and implement a process to build trust among your staff.

Trust is established and maintained through daily human interactions. Chapter 5 will help you know and grow your own communication skills through *empathic listening*, a vital aspect of improving principal support and retaining your teachers (Hughes, Matt, & O'Reilly, 2015). You will specifically learn how to listen to your teachers in a way that will help them feel heard.

Lasting impact in your school will only happen when the necessary inner work around authentic leadership, self-efficacy, and collective efficacy occurs with the help of healthy communication and trust. Our last chapter, chapter 6, unites the previous chapters as we address how to know and grow a compelling *vision* that lasts. We will explain how to get to know the personal visions of your staff, create a shared vision, and go beyond the crafting of a statement to ingrain the shared vision into your school.

This book is about now and the future. It is about recognizing and responding to the teacher retention problem in order to build a lasting legacy within the culture of your school. You'll find the heart of this book is built on familiar foundational leadership principles grounded in research and proven in practice. Yet, what makes this book distinct is how we use these principles to highlight the imperative role you play as a school leader, influencing the hearts, minds, and lives of those you are called to serve. To do this, we offer practical tools and suggestions meant to empower you, the school leader, to elevate your people, ultimately influencing their retention and the legacy you leave behind.

We wrote this book specifically for leaders and aspiring leaders working within the school setting, including principals, assistant principals, and those interested in school-level leadership. This book will remind veteran administrators why they initially went into school leadership, reinforce the great things they are already doing, and recharge their efforts toward making a long-lasting impact in the lives of their followers. For new school leaders, this book will act as a blueprint, helping them clarify their priorities as they begin their career in leadership and work on building their school's culture. We also recommend this book for district administrators as they support their school leaders in teacher retention efforts and seek to instill their own legacies within their school communities. While we approach each chapter through the lens of a building principal, several of the concepts we discuss throughout the book can be adjusted to many levels of educational leadership, from teacher leaders to superintendents.

Each chapter begins with a realistic leadership story—a challenging scenario that puts you in the shoes of a leadership dilemma. We then introduce and define an essential legacy-building concept and provide actionable ways to apply the concept in your setting. Throughout each chapter, we highlight relevant voices from the field of educational leadership. We also provide key considerations to think about when working with support staff, which we broadly define as any individual working within the school community, such as paraprofessionals, maintenance and custodial staff, secretaries, or food service staff. The What About the Support Staff? sections will give you action steps for acknowledging that your support staff play a key role in the culture of your school. Along the way, we interweave lessons, pragmatic philosophies, and stories from our own personal experiences as well as the experiences of those we have worked with from around the world. Halfway through each chapter, we've embedded a Three-Minute Pause—a place for you to stop, reflect on the concepts and ideas that have been introduced, make connections to prior knowledge or experiences, and seek clarification. Located at the end of each chapter is a rating tool you can use to reflect on your current state, highlight areas for progress, and challenge yourself to honestly assess if you've got the right motivation, values, and qualities to retain your teachers and build a lasting legacy. We conclude each chapter with a reflection guide for discussions. These guides are for collaborative teams, school- and district-level leadership teams, and book clubs to engage in supportive dialogue in regard to the concepts of each chapter. As you work through this book, we hope you feel empowered to know and grow yourself and your people and make a lasting impact on your school community and the individuals within it.

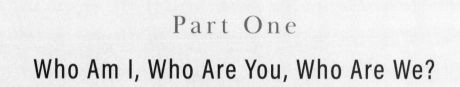

Part One

Who Am I, Who Are You, Who Are We?

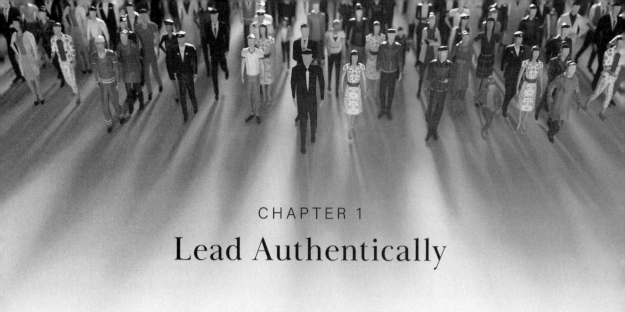

CHAPTER 1

Lead Authentically

Leadership is not simply something we do. It comes from somewhere inside us. Leadership is a process, an intimate expression of who we are. It is our being in action.

—Kevin Cashman

As the door slammed, Adam heard harsh words: "Either change your ways as an administrator, or I'm leaving." Hearing this from his most influential and trusted teacher tore Adam to the core and caused him to rethink his skills as principal of Edward Nash High School. Shocked and dismayed, Adam began to reflect on the circumstances that brought him to this moment.

He thought about his first days as principal leading Edward Nash High and the responsibilities and expectations that came with the position. He thought about his insecurities as he approached problem after problem, not always knowing what to do, not always having the right answer, and rarely feeling confident enough in himself to ask for help. The challenges he faced on a daily basis went well beyond anything he learned in leadership coursework. So, he worked harder, put in more hours, and was bound and determined to grow in his leadership capacity. But then his staff began to question his decision-making capabilities.

"Why aren't you suspending that student?"

"How can you give me instructional advice when you never actually taught mathematics?"

"Why can't you just listen to us?"

Adam struggled to answer questions like these, doubting his ability to be competent enough to be principal at Edward Nash High. To compensate for his lack of administrative leadership, he focused on his image, trying to live up to the pressure of how he and others thought he ought to be. He embodied a leadership persona driven by short-term personal victories, taking down anyone who got in his way. But, in doing so, he completely neglected the values that brought him into educational leadership in the first place—values like servanthood and empowering others. That's when the gap between who he was as a person compared to who he was as a leader began to widen, eventually leaving him guarded, defensive, and unable to fully open himself up to those around him. Now, thinking back, it was at that moment that the trust between Adam and his staff began to wane.

Adam would learn in the days and weeks to come that his inability to remain authentic to himself and to others was the underlying reason his superstar teacher threatened to leave the school. As a principal, there is little doubt your authenticity will have a dramatic impact on you and others, and if you change who you are to meet the challenges you face as a school leader, the consequences may be severe. Or, in the words of writer Eric Jackson (2014), "If you want to keep the most talented members of your team, it's time you started looking in the mirror and realize the biggest reasons why people quit have to do with you."

In this chapter, we delve into the question *Who am I?* as it relates to authentic leadership. We discuss what authentic leadership is and why it matters before discovering several strategies on how to become an authentic leader. You will then have the opportunity to assess your level of authentic leadership and reflect on the impact of your leadership on the wider school community.

What Is Authentic Leadership?

The innermost ripple of our Lasting Legacy model (figure 1.1) asks the question that is the focus of this chapter: "Who am I?" We believe the answer to this question will help you become a more authentic leader and will act as the premier catalyst for your faculty's belief in you, laying the groundwork for a sustained legacy. Lasting leadership must start from *within* the leader. In other words, you must realize who you are from within in order to understand how to lead authentically.

The roots of authenticity can be traced back to ancient Greek philosophy's short yet infamous phrase, "Know thyself." In his book *True North: Discover Your Authentic Leadership*, Bill George (2007) describes authentic leaders as:

> Genuine people who are true to themselves and to what they believe in. They engender trust and develop genuine connections with others. Because people trust them, they are able to motivate others to high levels

Figure 1.1: Lasting Legacy innermost ripple.

of performance. Rather than letting the expectations of other people guide them, they are prepared to be their own person and go their own way. As they develop as authentic leaders, they are more concerned about serving others than they are about their own success or recognition. (p. xxxi)

Scholars define authentic leadership in a variety of ways in their research. Bruce J. Avolio, William L. Gardner, Fred O. Walumbwa, Fred Luthans, and Douglas R. May (2004) say authentic leaders "know who they are, what they believe and value, and they act upon those values and beliefs while transparently interacting with others" (p. 802). Fred O. Walumbwa, Bruce J. Avolio, William L. Gardner, Tara S. Wernsing, and Suzanne J. Peterson (2008) describe an authentic leader as one who "promotes both positive psychological capacities and a positive ethical climate" (p. 94). We have adapted a definition of authentic leadership primarily from the three preceding definitions (Avolio et al., 2004; George, 2007; Walumbwa et al., 2008):

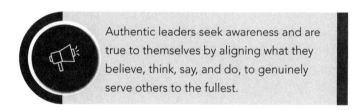

Authentic leaders seek awareness and are true to themselves by aligning what they believe, think, say, and do, to genuinely serve others to the fullest.

Answering the question Who am I? requires an understanding of what author Mark Hall (2014) calls our "roots and reach" (p. 18). Hall (2014) explains that, much like the roots of an old oak tree, there is a part of us far below the surface. The farther down we dig, the more we unearth the root of *who we are*—our core beliefs and values. There is also a visible part of us above the surface—our branches—revealed to the outside world. Our exposed branches dictate *how others see us*—our external behaviors, words, and expressions. When our roots take hold, we begin to have a greater understanding of who we are as people and what we can become as leaders. Our roots provide an anchor, helping us stand strong and holding us upright even through storms. When our roots grow and mature, our ability to stabilize and support the environment around us becomes more evident. Our roots provide steady and consistent support, never ceasing, never changing. Our branches are more adaptable, adjusting with the seasons. There are many parts to our branches—some strong, others weak. Our branches provide safety and security for those seeking shelter, and they can offer life to others (Hall, 2014). Healthy, authentic leadership requires depth and breadth in both roots and reach. For that to happen, our branches and our roots need to work in concert. What most people don't see is our roots are often just as big, if not bigger, than our branches. Our roots are what make our branches grow. As the reach of our branches grows, the more we are seen and the greater our capacity to influence those around us (Hall, 2014).

As the leader in your building, are you striving to align what you believe, think, say, and do? How healthy are your roots? Are your branches reaching others for good? Your authentic leadership will come from a conscious effort in growing both your roots and your reach.

Why Does Authentic Leadership Matter?

Inauthenticity results when leaders either intentionally or unintentionally allow their behaviors, circumstances, or pursuit of excellence to chart their course. But changing who you are as a leader to meet a current desire or need is neither productive nor healthy (Ribeiro, Duarte, & Filipe, 2018; Weiss, Razinskas, Backmann, & Hoegl, 2018). Your leadership should be authentic to you, not a persona that fits the current demand. In his book *Discover Your True North*, Bill George (2015) offers five common styles leaders may develop that take them off course, ultimately widening the gap between their authentic selves and their leadership selves. Can you relate your current leadership style or the leadership of those you've experienced in the past to any of the following examples? Leaders lacking in authenticity and who care more about their personal image than about reflecting who they truly are will be perceived as being disingenuous, possibly heading to problems in teacher retention. It's important to note, it is natural to feel elements of these styles within yourself. The way you process these feelings will serve as a guide in how you ultimately act. What matters most is your recognition of the difference between what you think as a leader and the actions you take.

- **Rationalizers** place blame on people, policies, and programs. Their primary goal is to accomplish short-term wins even if it means going against their own values in the process (George, 2015). Rationalizing principals leave little chance for teacher support and empowerment, and research suggests a lack of principal support is the teaching condition most related to teacher turnover (Carver-Thomas & Darling-Hammond, 2017).

- **Imposters** use politics to get where they are. They often act like confident leaders but are actually doubtful about their abilities, leaving them afraid that subordinates will catch on to them and take their jobs (George, 2015). Imposters are unwilling to provide shared leadership within the school and drive their teachers out of their buildings by limiting professional growth opportunities (Carver-Thomas & Darling-Hammond, 2017).

- **Glory seekers** want the spotlight and place great value on external rewards and self-recognition (George, 2015). Glory-seeking principals push initiatives for the benefit of their own self-interest, limiting teacher choice and voice. In turn, teachers who believe they have low levels of autonomy are less likely to stay in the teaching profession (Warner-Griffin, Cunningham, & Noel, 2018).

- **Shooting stars** are career driven, often living an unbalanced personal and professional life. A shooting star's goal is to climb the professional ladder. When they are given a chance to move into a higher position, they leave their current position without thinking twice (George, 2015). This is a problem for teacher retention, considering principal turnover is linked to higher rates of teacher turnover (Levin & Bradley, 2019).

- **Loners** believe they must lead alone, resulting in little shared leadership opportunities for teachers (George, 2015). Teachers want to have a part in school leadership, and the extent of their participation can influence their intent to stay in their position (Ingersoll & May, 2012).

THREE-MINUTE PAUSE

What are the amens, ahas, or ideas swirling in your brain about authentic leadership so far in this chapter?

_____

_____

_____

_____

_____

_____

_____

_____

How Do I Become an Authentic Leader?

Perhaps you've taken one or more of the five leadership paths outlined in the previous section and realized a few of the consequences that come with that. Or, maybe you've witnessed another educational leader veer off course. Regardless, you need tangible ways to know and grow yourself as an authentic school leader. In their theoretical model of authentic leadership, Walumbwa and colleagues (2008) offer four dimensions leaders can focus on to become more authentic: (1) self-awareness, (2) internalized moral perspective, (3) balanced processing, and (4) relational transparency. The remainder of this chapter addresses each of these four dimensions through a discussion of developing self-awareness, embracing core values, practicing authentic decision making, and increasing transparency with staff.

As we take a closer look at each dimension, you will find that you may be in the very beginning stages of one dimension while at the same time in the latter stages of another. At the end of this chapter, we offer a reflective tool to help you assess your current authentic leadership proficiency.

Develop Self-Awareness

Your day may start with three parent phone calls, settling a student bus conflict, wiping up a spill in the cafeteria, delivering announcements over the intercom, and participating in a meeting about an individualized education program (IEP), all before 8:30 a.m. While you may have good intentions, the reality is the demands of your school day often influence what you place your attention on in your school. These demands can cause you to lose focus on what matters most, pulling you away from the things you are really trying to accomplish as a school leader. This is no different for your authentic leadership. Before you know it, the business and busyness of the school day can cause you to lose sight of your authenticity as you move from task to task with little time to reflect on the impact of your leadership and how it aligns with who you are as a person. Authentic leadership requires deliberate practices of self-awareness before, during, and after the craziness of your days.

Self-awareness "refers to the extent to which leaders are aware of their own strengths, weaknesses, and motivations and of others' perceptions of their leadership" (Feng, 2016, p. 247). Your self-awareness illuminates the answer to the question "Who am I?" and will translate into the words you use and the actions you do or do not take in your school. A foundational element of self-awareness is recognizing your emotions and how others perceive them in a given situation (Miao, Humphrey, & Qian, 2018). For example, when was the last time an upset parent or teacher came to your office or classroom to discuss an issue that you disagreed with? Were you aware of how you were feeling and how you managed your emotions? Assessing yourself through a realistic lens can help you take note of your emotional state and respond appropriately.

Angel R. Dowden, Jeffrey M. Warren, and Hasseim Kambui (2014) offer a process you can use to develop your emotional self-awareness. The process follows three steps: (1) use frequent self-checks, (2) engage in positive self-talk when negative thoughts or feelings emerge, and (3) develop a habitual practice of self-journaling about your internal state (Dowden et al., 2014). While most of us pick and choose when and how we use these steps, research emphasizes the fundamental effectiveness of engaging in all three. Let's apply this to our example of an upset teacher coming into your office to discuss a disagreement.

1. **Use frequent self-checks:** Self-check by asking yourself, "How am I feeling about what this teacher is saying, and why am I feeling this way?" and "How may the teacher be receiving these feelings?"

2. **Engage in positive self-talk when negative thoughts or feelings emerge:** Dowden and colleagues (2014) suggest the use of "I" statements and flipping negative thoughts into positive ones. You may say to yourself, "I can learn from the perspective of this teacher. What must I do to ensure we come out of this conversation with a positive relationship and strengthened trust?"

3. **Develop a habitual practice of self-journaling about your internal state:** Write down your thoughts of how the conversation went, starting with a prompt such as, "The thoughts, emotions, and actions I had in my discussion with the teacher were . . ."

Increased self-awareness also requires knowing your personal strengths and areas of weakness (Eurich, 2018). Much like completing a comprehensive needs assessment for your school, you'll want to build knowledge of your strengths and weaknesses from multiple measures. Authors Terri L. Martin and Cameron L. Rains (2018) encourage leaders to develop their self-awareness by asking them to spend time self-reflecting, taking a personality inventory, and soliciting feedback from their colleagues and employees. You can do so by asking a variety of school stakeholders to complete a *360-degree feedback process* collecting their perceptions of your leadership (Kanaslan & Iyem, 2016). A 360-degree feedback process solicits anonymous perspectives from those within your school organization, including your immediate supervisors, peers, and those you supervise, and measures their perceptions of your strengths and areas for growth as a leader. The 360-degree feedback process is often used as a data collection tool, setting a baseline for professional growth goals. You could also use the "Strengths and Weaknesses Comparison Tool" found at the end of the chapter (page 28). We have found when leaders engage in this exercise, they deepen their understanding by formally discussing the results with others.

Leading with self-awareness creates the space for you to seek partnerships with those who compliment your areas of weakness. When you're open to learning from others, you ultimately find growth within yourself, further strengthening your leadership. For example, after receiving feedback on a strengths and weaknesses survey, principal Mary Anderson recognized her greatest area of weakness was preparing her staff to respond to the diverse needs of her school community. Mary sought the advice of a trusted mentor, who encouraged her to take into account the multiple perspectives of school and community stakeholders, listen to those perspectives with an open mind, and work to incorporate their ideas. As a result, she created *Better Together time*—time set aside each month to invite various stakeholders to share with her and her staff their lived experiences on timely educational topics such as diversity, homelessness, and mental health issues. Mary's staff embraced Better Together time as they began to understand in a new way the various barriers and needs of their students. In return, Mary's leadership strengthened as she found ways to complement her weaknesses with others' strengths.

Embrace Your Core Values

As the leader of a school building, you encounter endless decisions throughout your day. Some of those decisions will challenge your character and may require you to go against what other people think. This calls for both clarity and decisiveness on your part. During challenging circumstances, authentic leaders remain true to their convictions, relying on their leadership values to help guide their way (Viinamäki, 2012).

Embracing your core values helps you answer the question Who am I? through an internalized moral perspective. Arménio Rego, Filipa Sousa, Carla Marques, and Miguel Pina e Cunha (2012) consider an internalized moral perspective to be "the degree to which the leader sets a high standard for moral and ethical conduct, guides actions by internal moral standards and values . . . and expresses decision making and behaviors that are consistent with such internalized values" (p. 430). Think back to Bill George's (2015) five common leadership styles that were presented earlier in the chapter (page 14). Leadership styles go awry when personal values are not rooted. Your leadership intentions must be rooted in the values you hold. If you asked those leaders, "What are your leadership intentions?" how do you think they would respond? Better yet, how would you respond if we asked you? A fundamental component to your authentic leadership will be the values that guide your path. In fact, leaders should not lead *until* they have firm foundational values. Leaders embrace values when they are aware of their own values, live out their values in actionable ways, and when they realize how their values play a significant role in their leadership (Viinamäki, 2012).

Values can bring clarity to what is most important to your principalship and act as a guide to decision making. When you know what is most important to you, you can focus your attention on what matters most and go against the norm if necessary. For example, principals who value reflection time where they can center themselves often carve out time in the school day to do so regardless of external demands or requests. This practice grounds them, helping them be physically and emotionally present throughout the rest of the day. Importantly, having a set of core values makes your leadership style predictable, and it will influence the values you instill in your followers (van Niekerk & Botha, 2017).

Do you know what role your values currently play in your school leadership? You can assess this role by asking the following questions (Rego et al., 2012):

- "What are my moral and ethical expectations of my staff?"
- "How consistently do my daily actions and interactions align with the kind of person I believe I am?"
- "Do I make decisions based on the impact they will have on me and my school's future, or do I find quick fixes to current problems?"

The values you embrace have a significant impact on the way you approach your day. Realizing your strongest values is critical. Tapping into values in your leadership calls for an awareness of the values most important to you. To determine your prominent belief system, create a list containing no more than five core values. If you need help narrowing your list, consider the following questions, which we've adapted from Larry Ainsworth's (2013) recommendations to educators for identifying priority standards.

- Do your values have endurance?
- Do your values have leverage?
- Do your values have readiness for the next level?
- Do your values prepare you for the challenge ahead?

Establish routines and rituals that remind you of your core values throughout the school day. Make your values visible. For example, write them down on a sticky note by your computer, set them as a reminder on your phone, or display them as artwork in your office.

Leading with a set of core values requires living them out so others can see them. For example, superintendent Ed Richardson lived out his core values of family, community, profession, and appreciation of others by creating the "Oh My Pineapple" award. This tradition started as a private family saying and became a public award by which Ed honored incredible displays of character. He gave students, staff, and community members full-sized pineapples celebrating their ability to stand tall on the outside and stay sweet on the inside. The pineapple soon became a symbol to rally behind, and his core values became ingrained in the community.

As you begin to identify what your values look like, sound like, and feel like under your leadership, use the "Leadership Values Reflection Template" reproducible at the end of the chapter (page 29), a template inspired by Dr. Ed Richardson, to help frame how you will live out your values on a daily basis.

INSIGHTS FROM THE FIELD

"Before becoming an educational leader, I wish I had known just how thick my skin was going to need to be. An educational leader must be prepared to do the right thing each and every time. It's not hard wanting to do the right thing; it's hard knowing someone is not going to be happy with your decision, and you may not be able to tell your side or all of the story.

Integrity is critical to doing the right thing. Over time, people will come to appreciate your consistent integrity, but, oh, is it hard in the moment! Do it all with the best interests of the students in mind. Love people, even those that don't love you back. Lean on your networks, and never regret doing the right thing!"

—Superintendent,
personal communication, June 26, 2020

Practice Authentic Decision Making

Developing self-awareness and knowing your values are important internal aspects of authenticity, but authentic leadership occurs only when who you are on the inside aligns with your external behaviors on the outside. Taking the time to consciously connect your heart with your hand or your values with your actions provides visible authenticity for your teachers to see (Sergiovanni & Green, 2015). James A. Autry (as cited in Marzano, Warrick, Rains, & DuFour, 2018) explains the need for visible authenticity from a leader by recognizing and appreciating those within your building:

> [Teachers] can determine who you are only by observing what you do. They can't see inside your head, they can't know what you think or how you feel, they can't subliminally detect your compassion or pain or joy or goodwill. In other words, the only way you can manifest your character, your personhood, and your spirit in the workplace is through your behavior. (p. 20)

As a school principal, this means an important part of your leadership is *showing* your authenticity. A good starting point for principals is to approach difficult decisions with an objective lens through authentic decision making. We refer to *authentic decision making* as a school leader's ability to remain open-minded, seeking to understand varying viewpoints and perspectives before making a decision (Hirst, Walumbwa, Aryee, Butarbutar, & Chen, 2016).

A term often referenced with such a decision-making process is *balanced processing* (Miao et al., 2018). When school leaders make authentic decisions, they process pertinent data, then balance their perceptions with those that challenge their current beliefs and assumptions (Duncan, Green, Gergen, & Ecung, 2017). A principal we know takes this one step further by suggesting we include the understanding of our inherent bias into our decision-making equation. According to principal Scott Dart, we should ask ourselves, "How does my inherent bias figure into how I lead? Do I listen to others? Do I take the time to understand where others are coming from?" (S. Dart, personal communication, June 23, 2020). If you follow a balanced decision-making process, will your teachers always agree with you? Not always, but consistently remaining objective will model your willingness to approach difficult decisions from all angles.

Consider this scenario. Several of your elementary students are responsible for getting themselves ready in the morning and arriving at the bus stop on their own. However, a number of them are unable to do this consistently, causing them to be late to school or absent for the day. At the same time, student needs are high and achievement numbers are low in your building, and additional support staff could help alleviate some of the pressure teachers feel. You've found enough funding to either pay for a late bus to pick up students that missed the first bus or to pay for one part-time support staff member. You assume your teaching staff will be split on the decision you make, as pockets of teacher groups have approached you with what they believe is the best decision. However, assumptions are not enough to support an authentic decision-making process. So, how do you remain objective and honor the multiple opinions of others, while at the same time staying true to your core values? Figure 1.2 (page 22) models how we would approach this scenario through balanced processing. A blank template of this figure, which you can use when encountering your own decision-making situations, can be found at the end of the chapter (page 30). (As a side note, there are times when leaders must make decisions without the perspectives of others. If you already know what the decision will be, do not ask for input. It's better to not ask at all than to ask when you really don't mean it or need it.)

Steps for Authentic Decision Making	Things to Consider	Check Here After Completing Each Step
What decision do you need to make?	Should our school fund a late bus to pick up absent students or hire one additional, part-time support staff member?	
What data must you analyze to make an informed decision?	Student attendance data Student behavior data State assessment data Parent, staff, and student surveys	
What do you believe is the right decision?	To fund a late bus to pick up absent students	
How do your values, biases, and assumptions play into your thinking?	The attendance rate is important because students are more likely to succeed in academics when they attend school consistently. It's difficult for the teacher and the class to build their skills and progress if students are frequently absent. In addition to falling behind in academics, students who are not in school on a regular basis are more likely to get into trouble with the law and cause problems in their communities.	
Which people do you need to hear from who have a different opinion than you? What are their perspectives?	I need to hear from staff whom this affects. This would include the intervention specialists. Their perspective is that a multitiered system of supports (MTSS) helps schools to organize levels of supports based on intensity so that students receive necessary instruction, support, and interventions based on need. This helps educators to respond appropriately and provide students with the assistance they need to prosper in the classroom. Each licensed staff member is essential in providing the necessary support for the students.	
How will you approach asking others for their perspectives?	Ask: "I'd like to get your perspective on something. But before I do that, I want to be crystal-clear that I'm not sure which direction we're going to go. I'm not necessarily looking for a solution. I just know your input is valuable, and your perspective will help me understand this situation better before I make a decision. Just so you know, my decision may not be exactly what you are hoping for, but I will communicate my decision as soon as it's appropriate. I will be upfront and honest with you about the decision I make."	

What is the decision you made?	Fund a late bus to pick up absent students.	
What are the reasons for your decision? (Be sure to include reasons outside of your own personal beliefs.)	By funding the late bus, students are more likely to keep up with daily lessons and assignments and take quizzes and tests on time. Research has shown that students' regular attendance may be the greatest factor influencing their academic success. When students attend school regularly, they may not need additional support.	
How will you communicate your decision to all stakeholders? (Consider your approach to those who both agree and disagree with you.)	The leadership team will share the decision at a staff meeting along with talking points for the staff to share in their communication with families. The building principal will share this information with the parents and families through the monthly newsletter, at the monthly PTA meeting, at the monthly coffee and conversation with the principal, and at local community outreach meetings.	

Sources: Adapted from Duncan et al., 2017; Hirst et al., 2016; Miao et al., 2018.

Figure 1.2: Authentic decision-making checklist example.

Increase Transparency With Your Staff

Your staff want to feel in on things. They want to know you are providing them relevant information with openness, honesty, and respect. They also want to know who you are as a person, what you're thinking, and how you feel things are going. You may think you have a grasp on your authentic self, but if you can't be transparent with your staff, they will believe you have something to hide. Low transparency produces low trust. Low trust produces low results. On the flip side, relational transparency is your authenticity accelerator, building trust and showing staff your human side.

Relational transparency is the willingness to open yourself up to others. When you are transparent with your staff, you do not hesitate to give them information when they need it, and you are ready and willing to share your true perspective if necessary (Rego et al., 2012). Your openness may be school-related or personal, positive or negative, triumphant or embattled. Regardless, the most important aspect of relational transparency is aligning the values you hold with an open line of communication to staff.

Two common ways principals are transparent with their teachers are when they admit their mistakes and when they ask for help. Most teachers can share examples of times they wished their principal had apologized for a mistake they made. For example, one new elementary school principal mandated a new discipline policy, unintentionally undermining the work done prior to his tenure. When the principal admitted to trying to implement the policy too fast, the teaching staff felt the principal could look beyond himself and empathize with the situation. The staff quickly moved forward, collecting relevant data, building shared knowledge, and establishing a discipline task force.

Another middle school principal demonstrated transparency when she recruited staff members to help her with a districtwide MTSS initiative. This principal used a staff meeting to share the purpose of the initiative and the strengths she felt she had in leading organizational change. She also admitted to her uneasiness with the topic and asked for staff volunteers who could complement her strengths with their knowledge of MTSS. Her awareness of her own strengths and weaknesses allowed her to be relationally transparent, providing opportunities for others to use their own strengths.

To make transparent communication a habitual practice, principals should intentionally embed their transparency into pre-established routines such as weekly newsletters and staff meetings. Figure 1.3 is an example of transparent communication from a superintendent to his staff.

To: Staff
From: Superintendent Martinson
Subject: First Week

I hope this email finds you at the end of a great first week with all of the kids back!

I've been asked how things are going on my end. I struggle with an answer, as it's been hard to wrap my mind around how I feel. I think I've narrowed it down to: humbling.

Stepping into the role of superintendent has been a humbling experience.

Lots of "I thought I knew" moments, from how our district operates to how different individuals and departments impact us as a whole. I've had a lot of eye-opening "I thought I knew" moments. I mean that in the most positive of ways.

Each and every one of us holds a very important piece of the Independent School District 318 puzzle. Each and every one of us walks our daily miles in our own shoes, and in those daily miles, many of us are experiencing things that no one else will ever know. And in that, it's humbling to realize, "I thought I knew, but I don't." I don't know what each and every person does in our district or is going through in our district. From the heart, though, I can say thank you, thank you for trying to make each day a great day (and thank you for your patience as I, too, navigate my position in the district).

Please continue to do your best. If your today is even just a little better than your yesterday, imagine how great your tomorrows will be!

Have a great weekend, everyone.

—Sean

Figure 1.3: Superintendent's letter to staff.

On occasion, your staff will need you to exude confidence, resolve, or optimism regardless of your personal feelings. Ideally, authentic leaders would exhibit candor with all stakeholders, but in reality, it's not always appropriate to do this. There are times when our hearts are with our staff, but our minds are elsewhere concerned about personal or professional experiences unrelated to the immediate needs of the staff. Showing your humanness connects you to your staff, but there is a balancing act between what you personally need and what your staff need to be successful. We recommend you find a mentor or a group of trusted individuals you can contact to ask questions, share successes, and discuss struggles. You may find these people within your own district, in a regional cohort of school leaders, or on an online social media platform.

"An authentic leader is someone who is a servant leader, leading with grace, compassion, and transparency. They are someone who is willing to listen and learn, who allows others with expertise to lead. I wish I learned to ask more questions upfront and to accept mentorship from someone who had come before me. Being able to have that touchpoint is extremely important in the area of growth. Though I cannot be immune to all leadership problems, I can be assisted in the hope of having guidance to navigate foreseeable issues."

—Teacher leader,
personal communication, June 22, 2020

Reflection

You will find the "Establishing Authentic Leadership Rating Scale" reproducible at the end of the chapter (page 31). The rating scale will help you assess your current state of authentic leadership, identify areas of strength and needs for improvement, and provide focus to your professional learning progress.

> ## What About the Support Staff?
> - Demonstrate genuine caring by taking an interest in the lives of staff members, asking them questions, and connecting with them. In turn, share your own personal goals, values, and aspirations.
> - Model what you expect from your support staff. You have to be the boots on the ground, seeking to understand their experiences from their points of view. You can do this by spending time doing what they do with them.
> - Give support staff grace, assuming they have good intentions until you've been proven otherwise. Continue to coach, model, build up, and provide training.

Conclusion

Throughout this chapter we encouraged you to reflect inward as you asked the question, "Who am I?" Developing your own roots and reach are the first two vital steps in teacher retention and legacy building. Authentic leadership allows you to understand yourself and begin to look outward by asking "Who are you?" to your teachers. Without experiencing your authenticity as their leader, your teachers will never fully grasp the enormity of their own roots and reach.

Most of your teachers will never know your search for self-awareness, how you defined your values, practiced authentic decision making, or worked toward greater relational transparency, but your authenticity will be felt by your teachers and have an impact on their retention, creating your lasting legacy.

Talk It Over: Reflection Guide for Discussions

Growing as a learner and leader takes thoughtful reflection. Interacting with this book's text and listening to the experiences of others will make you more fully aware of who you are as a leader and the steps you can take to grow. Thoughtful conversations take time and energy, but investing in each other through conversation will establish the support group you will need when the going gets tough.

1. **Introducing yourself to the topic:** Have you witnessed any authentic leaders in your life? How have you experienced these people's leadership? How do they stand out differently from other leaders?

2. **Looking inward:** By observing other authentic leaders, how has your outlook toward leadership changed?

3. **Making connections:** Take a moment to interact with the following statement by highlighting, underlining, or writing in the margins. Jot down questions or connections that you have with the statement to your life, community, and world. Then, share out your thoughts.

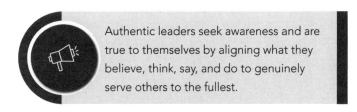

Authentic leaders seek awareness and are true to themselves by aligning what they believe, think, say, and do to genuinely serve others to the fullest.

4. **Applying it in practice:** Growing as a leader takes steps of action. You can do that with confidence when you share openly with others, supporting one another in those steps. Reflect on the "Establishing Authentic Leadership Rating Scale" (page 31). Where is your greatest need for growth? What step will you take to grow in that area?

Strengths and Weaknesses Comparison Tool

Step 1: What are my strengths and weaknesses?	Step 2: What does a personality inventory identify as my strengths and weaknesses?	Step 3: What does a colleague or employee identify as my strengths and weaknesses?
Strengths	**Strengths**	**Strengths**
1. 2. 3.	1. 2. 3.	1. 2. 3.
Weaknesses	**Weaknesses**	**Weaknesses**
1. 2. 3.	1. 2. 3.	1. 2. 3.

Step 4:

In what ways are my lists alike?

In what ways are my lists different?

My biggest takeaway from reflecting on the three lists is:

Source: Adapted from Martin, T. L., & Rains, C. L. (2018). Stronger together: Answering the questions of collaborative leadership. Bloomington, IN: Solution Tree Press.

Leadership Values Reflection Template

Value	What does it look like?	What does it sound like?	What does it feel like?
1.			
2.			
3.			

Authentic Decision Making Through Balanced Processing Checklist

Steps for Authentic Decision Making	Things to Consider	Check Here After Completing Each Step
What decision do you need to make?		
What data must you analyze to make an informed decision?		
What do you believe is the right decision?		
How do your values, biases, and assumptions play into your thinking?		
Which people do you need to hear from who have a different opinion than you? What are their perspectives?		
How will you approach asking others for their perspectives?		
What is the decision you made?		
What are the reasons for your decision? (Be sure to include reasons outside of your own personal beliefs.)		
How will you communicate your decision to all stakeholders? (Consider your approach to those who both agree and disagree with you.)		

Sources: Adapted from Duncan, P., Green, M., Gergen, E., & Ecung, W. (2017). Authentic leadership—is it more than emotional intelligence? Administrative Issues Journal, 7*(2), 11–22; Hirst, G., Walumbwa, F., Aryee, S., Butarbutar, I., & Chen, C. J. H. (2016). A multi-level investigation of authentic leadership as an antecedent of helping behavior.* Journal of Business Ethics, 139*(3), 485–499; Miao, C., Humphrey, R. H., & Qian, S. (2018). Emotional intelligence and authentic leadership: A meta-analysis.* Leadership and Organization Development Journal, 39*(5), 679–690.*

Establishing Authentic Leadership Rating Scale

Read each statement and reflect on how you rate your authenticity. Then, determine next steps for growth in your authentic leadership.

Developing Self-Awareness	Strongly Disagree	Somewhat Disagree	Somewhat Agree	Strongly Agree
I self-check and respond to situations fully aware of my thoughts, feelings, and actions.				
Next Steps:				
I engage in self-talk when negative or detrimental thinking patterns emerge.				
Next Steps:				
I implement habitual practices of self-awareness such as journaling.				
Next Steps:				
I reflect on my personal strengths and weaknesses using multiple methods of assessment.				
Next Steps:				

page 1 of 3

Embracing Your Core Values	Strongly Disagree	Somewhat Disagree	Somewhat Agree	Strongly Agree
I can identify specific ways my values influence my leadership.				
Next Steps:				
I have a list of core leadership values.				
Next Steps:				
I know what each of my values looks like, sounds like, and feels like in my leadership.				
Next Steps:				

Practicing Authentic Decision Making	Strongly Disagree	Somewhat Disagree	Somewhat Agree	Strongly Agree
I analyze relevant data prior to making a difficult decision.				
Next Steps:				
I seek multiple perspectives prior to making a difficult decision.				
Next Steps:				

Increasing Transparency With Staff	Strongly Disagree	Somewhat Disagree	Somewhat Agree	Strongly Agree
I practice transparency that is aligned to my core values.				
Next Steps:				
I seek help when needed.				
Next Steps:				
I admit to my mistakes.				
Next Steps:				

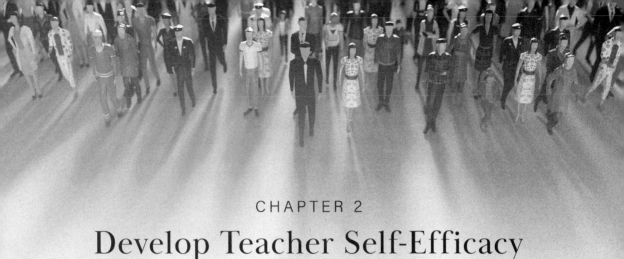

CHAPTER 2

Develop Teacher Self-Efficacy

*Leaders become great, not because of
their power, but because of their ability to
empower others.*

—John Maxwell

One decision is all it takes. One seemingly common decision in a life filled with decisions. In 2016, one decision would make all the difference in the world—a difference that would determine the career trajectories of Sarah and her twin sister Beth. This decision to work as second-grade teachers in neighboring elementary schools would jumpstart the foundation of Sarah's vocational pursuits, but it would stop Beth's career right in its tracks.

The differences between the two schools, the one where Beth worked and the one where Sarah worked, were hardly noticeable, really—little things kept the schools from being exactly alike. But in the end, isn't it the little things that make all the difference? For Sarah, many little things jump-started her career. She met with her principal before the start of the year. She was paired with a mentor upon hire who encouraged her and whom she relied on as her first point of contact to explain instructional practices, provide emotional support, and develop classroom resources. Sarah's mentor also motivated her to build other trusting relationships in the school. Beth's experiences, on the other hand, created standstills in her career development. Beth never met with her principal, never had a mentor, and never developed significant relationships with anyone from the school. Instead, prior to the first day of school, Beth received a letter from an administrative assistant explaining school logistics.

Not long into the school year, Sarah's professional career in education began to take hold. Sarah's mentor facilitated her transition into a schoolwide professional learning community (PLC) as a member of a grade-level collaborative team. With little experience, Sarah leaned heavily on her team and the broader PLC culture for teaching strategies and classroom management techniques. Beth wasn't as lucky. She longed for this type of collaboration—colleagues with whom to develop lesson plans, analyze data, and determine next steps in teaching. However, there was no one. Beth felt alone, abandoned, frustrated, and confused. Many of her colleagues kept to themselves, having little time, patience, or energy for Beth, the new kid. If Beth were to survive her first year of teaching, she would have to accomplish this on her own.

Like many first-year teachers, by midyear, Sarah and Beth were struggling to balance the challenges of teaching. Sarah's principal and mentor were cognizant of this and ramped up her support with professional development tailored specifically to her needs. Beth's principal took a different approach. He highlighted each competency she was not meeting sufficiently and encouraged her to attend a workshop over the summer to become a better teacher.

By the end of the year, Sarah had received enough critical support and guidance to help her incrementally grow into a stronger teacher with a bright future ahead. Beth continued to receive little support, little guidance, and little chance of surviving the teaching profession. In fact, it didn't take long for Beth to conclude the demands of the teaching profession were too immense for her abilities. For Beth, it felt like the only thing she could do was quit, but she really just needed better supports as part of a healthy school culture.

Each year, teachers across the country decide whether or not to remain in the teaching profession. Some, like Sarah, don't think twice. They continue to teach because they believe it is their calling and something they were born to do. Some, like Beth, believe otherwise, leaving a profession that gave them little more than a jaded perspective of the current educational reality.

Have you ever wondered why teachers with seemingly similar backgrounds, educational experiences, salaries, and school characteristics choose to leave while others choose to stay? The answer lies in the simple yet profound truth: *teacher self-efficacy matters*.

In this chapter, we take a deep look at teacher self-efficacy. We discuss what self-efficacy is and why it matters before discovering several strategies on how you can develop teacher self-efficacy. You will then have the opportunity to assess your current abilities in developing teacher self-efficacy and reflect on the impact of your leadership on the wider school community.

What Is Self-Efficacy?

Each and every one of your teachers wants to be accepted and valued for who they are. They strive to make notable contributions to their calling and aspire to belong to something greater than themselves. Each and every one of your teachers has something unique to bring to your school community—a genuine strength of talent, skill, or ability. When you get to know who your teachers are and what makes them unique, you can help them believe in themselves and their capabilities. In this chapter, we take a closer look at the second ripple of our Lasting Legacy model by asking the question "Who are you?" (see figure 2.1). The answer to this question can make a difference in the lives of your teachers as it will give you insight into the beliefs and practices your teachers need so they can believe in themselves and the strengths they already possess. In other words, when you know who your teachers are, you can help elevate their self-efficacy, a key factor in teacher retention.

Figure 2.1: The second ripple in the Lasting Legacy model.

Psychologist Albert Bandura (1993) originated the construct of self-efficacy and defines it as "people's beliefs about their capabilities to exercise control over their own level of functioning and over events that affect their lives" (p. 118). He claims individuals' efficacy beliefs "influence how people feel, think, motivate themselves, and behave" (p. 118). Your teacher's self-efficacy will dictate the experiences they choose to embrace along with:

> the challenges and goals they set for themselves and their commitment to them, how much effort they put forth in given endeavors, the outcomes they expect their efforts to produce, how long they persevere in the face of obstacles, their resilience to adversity, the quality of their emotional life and how much stress and depression they experience in coping with taxing environmental demands, and the life choices they make and the accomplishments they realize. (Bandura, 2006, p. 309)

Bandura (1994) suggests four sources of self-efficacy.

1. **Mastery experiences:** For teachers to believe in their capabilities, they need to experience success and overcome setbacks. Leaders should give teachers several opportunities to master certain tasks

while simultaneously supporting them and pushing their limits to try new things.

2. **Vicarious experiences:** Teachers are more likely to believe in their own capacity when they see others work hard and succeed in similar areas. Leaders should provide teachers the time and resources to observe and learn from role models similar to themselves.

3. **Social persuasion:** The words you speak to your teachers act as critical elements to teacher self-efficacy. When teachers *hear* they have what it takes, with proper support and guidance, they are more likely to *believe* they have what it takes.

4. **Physiological state:** Personal moods and feelings influence perceptions of self-efficacy. Teachers rely partly on their state of mental health to determine whether or not they are capable of completing a task. Self-efficacy improves when leaders establish environments supportive of the emotional and physical states of their teachers.

Research suggests the use of Bandura's (1994) four sources of self-efficacy plays a major role in establishing positive teacher outcomes related to teacher retention, such as job satisfaction (Aldridge & Fraser, 2016), commitment (Demir, 2020), and reduced burnout (Smetackovaa, 2017). Take, for instance, the role self-efficacy plays in teacher burnout. Authors Christina Maslach and Michael P. Leiter (2016) define burnout as "a psychological syndrome emerging from a prolonged response to chronic interpersonal stressors on the job" (p. 103). As teachers burn out, they respond by experiencing three specific dimensions: (1) exhaustion, (2) depersonalization, and (3) reduced personal accomplishment (Maslach & Leiter, 2016). However, self-efficacy acts as a natural buffer between the daily persistent stressors teachers feel and their experience of each burnout dimension (Weibenfels, Benick, & Perels, 2021). In other words, a strong sense of self-efficacy reduces the chances for burnout even when a teacher is excessively stressed.

Consider the example of a teacher who is working with a physically aggressive student, a task associated with needing high levels of self-efficacy (Lai, Li, Ji, Wong, & Lo, 2016). The persistent behavior of that student may display as a daily stressor for your teacher. If your teachers' self-efficacy is low, they will be more likely to withdraw from their current situation (depersonalization), become unproductive and lose heart while failing to attain desired goals (reduced personal accomplishment), and have little energy to keep going (exhaustion). On the other hand, if their self-efficacy is high, your teachers may view their stress as something to learn from or a temporary bump in the road, only delaying their eventual accomplishments.

The school leader's role in all of this is to use Bandura's (1994) four sources of self-efficacy as a lens to look through, observing the world through your teachers' needs. As you observe the needs of your teachers, you will identify the source or sources of efficacy that align with what they need the most. In the case of the teacher working with a physically aggressive student, you may need to help develop their self-efficacy through social persuasion, telling that teacher they are doing the right things to support that student and to not give up. It could be that your teacher needs to vicariously learn from another model teacher in a similar situation to see how their peer handles daily challenges. You may need to check in on the physiological state of your teacher, supporting their mental health and well-being. Or, your teacher may need mastery learning experiences with built-in short-term goals as they work toward mastering specific teaching techniques. Regardless of the specific stressors your teachers face, the key for you as leader is to understand their specific self-efficacy needs and to find ways to support those needs. It is inevitable that at one point or another your teachers will encounter stressful situations and you'll need to find ways to support them. Bandura's (1994) four sources of self-efficacy prove to be a viable option.

Why Does Teacher Self-Efficacy Matter?

There is little doubt developing teacher self-efficacy is a proactive approach for leaders to help their teachers face, overcome, and thrive through the hardest days of teaching. When your teachers exhibit a strong sense of self-efficacy, they are more likely to believe in themselves and their capabilities no matter the challenges set before them. This means regardless of the physical, social, emotional, and psychological challenges related to the teaching profession, developing the self-efficacy of teachers is a major component to teacher retention. Much as it was for Sarah in this chapter's opening story, when teachers are given the kinds of support that will enhance their self-efficacy throughout the school year, they are more likely to find success even when things are difficult, and in turn are more likely to stay in their teaching positions (Afzal, Arshad, Saleem, & Farooq, 2019). For Sarah, those supports came in the form of a master mentor, a strong schoolwide professional learning community, professional development tailored to her needs, and a building principal who checked in with her regularly. Supports such as these act as a type of safety net for teachers, ready to catch them as they encounter difficult times that may compromise their beliefs in themselves. As leaders, we thoughtfully put in place self-efficacy building supports so teachers just like Sarah can lean on these supports when they feel like they are going to fall or fail. Knowing they have supports to lean on can elevate teachers' levels of job satisfaction and commitment (Demir, 2020), further enhancing the chance of their retention (Okubanjo, 2014).

It is critical that you are aware of the types of teacher supports you are using in light of what educational research suggests about developing teacher self-efficacy. As leaders, we need to know the mechanisms most beneficial to helping teachers believe in themselves and how to use those mechanisms in the right way. Additionally, researchers in the field of educational leadership highlight the pressing need to retain teachers as a warning for principals to consider the way they approach their leadership (Carver-Thomas & Darling-Hammond, 2017), and ultimately how they support their teachers.

If you want to develop the self-efficacy of your teachers, then you must prioritize the needs of your teachers before your own. Traditionally, school organizations take the shape of a hierarchical triangle with the leader at the top, creating systems, protocols, and procedures that influence the day-to-day realities of those who sit below them: teachers, students, and staff. By flipping that model upside down, you essentially find ways to lift others up, setting aside your personal agenda for the betterment of your people. In such a school, you as the leader serve your people by providing enough critical and scaffolded support that your teachers have within themselves the ability to say, "I can do this!" well beyond your principal tenure. This type of leadership, servant leadership, is a promising leadership style conducive to supporting and ultimately retaining teachers (Shaw & Newton, 2014). Servant leadership is distinctly different from several other forms of leadership, in that a servant leader's primary focus is the success and well-being of their people (Eva, Robin, Sendjaya, van Dierendonck, & Liden, 2019). In his seminal book *The Servant as Leader,* Robert K. Greenleaf (1970) coins the term *servant leader* and goes on to explain how servant leadership differs from all others:

> The difference manifests itself in the care taken by the servant—first to make sure that other people's highest priority needs are being served. The best test, and difficult to administer, is: do those served grow as persons; do they, *while being served,* become healthier, wiser, freer, more autonomous, more likely themselves to become servants? *And,* what is the effect on the least privileged in society; will he benefit or at least not be further deprived? (p. 10)

Research emphasizes the fact that when school leaders embody the concepts of servant leadership, they completely revolutionize what it means to lead a school, positively transforming the school and the teachers working within it (Shaw & Newton, 2014; Turkmen & Gul, 2017). Consider the example of Sarah's principal from the opening story in this chapter. This principal thoughtfully put in place a system of supports for Sarah, knowing her first year of teaching would be difficult. But, he also artfully orchestrated a delicate balancing act between standing back and stepping in. At times, he stood back and allowed Sarah to work through the discomfort of challenging circumstances, knowing her discomfort would eventually lead to growth. When this happened, he empowered others within Sarah's circle of influence to play a role in her development. At other times, he stepped in and provided additional support for Sarah, knowing her success at that moment hinged on his ability to utilize the resources at his disposal that she needed to succeed. For servant leaders like Sarah's principal, leading is about much more than teaching and learning, leading is about the selfless pursuit of developing *people,* enriching their lives and supporting them to become the best version of themselves.

INSIGHTS FROM THE FIELD

"The one thing that I wish I knew prior to becoming an administrator was just how powerful a group of teachers can be. Whether in small groups or an entire faculty, teachers are where the rubber meets the road in education. Of course, we need to be student centered, but to achieve the best that schools can, we need to be teacher focused as well. Empowering those who directly work with our students is the foundation to experiencing positive movement in helping our students learn to the best of their abilities."

—Assistant principal,
personal communication, July 10, 2020

THREE-MINUTE PAUSE

What are the amens, ahas, or ideas swirling in your brain about developing self-efficacy in others so far in this chapter?

_____

_____

_____

_____

_____

_____

_____

_____

_____

How Do I Develop Teacher Self-Efficacy?

Teacher self-efficacy proves to be a promising contributing factor to keeping your teachers in the classroom. As a building leader, do you know what it will take to elevate and maintain your teachers' beliefs about their own capabilities? Are you leading in a way that will help your people grow into healthier, wiser, freer, more autonomous teachers who will carry your legacy *within* them? Do you know how to develop teacher self-efficacy? Bandura's (1994) four sources of self-efficacy—mastery experiences, vicarious experiences, social persuasion, and physiological state—should be an inherent aspect of planning for and providing supports for your teachers. The remainder of this chapter incorporates these four sources and explores three ways to support your teachers and develop their self-efficacy. The three ways include: (1) providing high-impact teacher induction, (2) implementing job-embedded professional development, and (3) creating self-efficacious working conditions.

Provide High-Impact Teacher Induction

We begin our discussion with a vital component of retaining early career teachers: providing high-impact teacher induction. Research suggests teachers encounter several challenges during the first year of their job. These include minimal classroom and time-management skills, insufficient curriculum and instruction practices, and limited administrative and colleague support (Dias-Lacy & Guirguis, 2017). For early career teachers to understand how to become outstanding teachers, they need strategically planned vicarious experiences to *show* them how to do things.

Planning vicarious experiences for new teachers using the teacher induction process can increase teacher self-efficacy. However, several of the current induction programs across the country do little to develop self-efficacy in our teachers (Goldrick, 2016). Instead, many schools employ a cross-it-off-the-list method of induction. Typically, this type of induction program consists of an orientation day at the start of the school year and the pairing of a mentor. Mentor-mentee partnerships then perform the necessary tasks in order to cross them off the list as something to get done, only for mentors and mentees to then return to their respective classrooms to get back to the real work of teaching. Consider your current induction program and if it centers on providing self-efficacy-building experiences for your teachers or if it follows more of a cross-it-off-the-list method of teacher induction.

PLC at Work® architects and experts Richard DuFour, Rebecca DuFour, Robert Eaker, Thomas W. Many, and Mike Mattos (2016) call for a thoughtfully planned system of induction, one in which "people throughout the school work together in an intentional, coordinated way to achieve the goal of greater teacher retention" (p. 193). A high-quality and effective induction program must have built-in layers of self-efficacy support.

Teachers should receive vicarious experiences from multiple individuals within the school. This type of induction program would include four components.

1. **An orientation session for new teachers:** There is no better time to introduce your new teachers to the culture of your school than before the school year starts. This is also the first time to ask the question "Who are you?" to new staff. Your orientation session should have two purposes: (1) to build relational capacity and (2) to provide initial vicarious learning experiences. Set aside time for teachers to share about themselves. Have role model teachers help facilitate the day. Choose role models you believe your new teachers should watch and learn from. Vicarious learning works best when teachers can see themselves in those doing the modeling (Bandura, 1994). Share your staff's collective commitments to teaching to define for your new staff what success looks like in the school, giving a visual for your new teachers to strive toward. A few collective commitments one principal shares with each of his incoming staff members include:

   • We believe all kids have the capacity to learn and grow academically, socially, and emotionally. We take pride in understanding each individual student's unique attributes and consider the gifts all kids bring to our school as valuable.

   • Our building climate is key to the success of our students and staff. Therefore, it is important that we foster a positive attitude.

   • We believe in the importance of a committed team. Therefore, it is important to be an active participant within the team. PLCs, staff meetings, grade-level meetings, sharing, participation on building teams, and being a contributor are all attributes of our team's success (R. DeBay, personal communication, June 30, 2020).

2. **A qualified mentor:** A highly qualified mentor is imperative to improving new teacher self-efficacy. Consider mentors in your school as the primary vicarious learning models for your new teachers. New teachers watch mentors formally and informally, learning by the way they approach and respond to challenges throughout the day. Strong mentors have a high sense of self-efficacy in curriculum, instruction, and classroom management and are willing to work with their mentees as adult learners (Goldrick, 2016). While research suggests mentees should be paired with mentors from the same field (Ingersoll & Strong, 2011), consider the individual needs of both the mentor and mentee, including personality and work-related goals. Further, effective mentorships require

uninterrupted collaboration time for as much as one to two hours each week (Goldrick, 2016).

3. **A collaborative team:** Operating with the framework of a collaborative team, whether based on grade level, content area, or some other construct, allows new teachers to learn vicariously by watching master teachers support student learning by designing curriculum and instruction plans, strategically developing common formative assessments, and collaborating about student learning data to inform future instruction. When collaborative teams act as part of a broader, school- or districtwide PLC, they further "expand the sources of support for beginning teachers beyond the individual mentor and the individual school" (Goldrick, 2016).

4. **Personalized professional development experiences:** Teachers have varying professional development needs, requiring a differentiation in learning experiences. You can personalize your new teachers' professional development by allotting time for new teachers to observe and learn in areas where they feel less capable. For instance, a new science teacher may have a low sense of efficacy in facilitating field investigations. To develop their self-efficacy, you could plan for them to observe an experienced science teacher successfully facilitating a field investigation.

Implement Job-Embedded Professional Development

A major component of teacher self-efficacy development is the participation in mastery experiences. Teachers need time and support to *practice* good teaching within the context of the teaching day. Andrew Croft, Jane G. Coggshall, Megan Dolan, and Elizabeth Powers (2010) define job-embedded professional development as "teacher learning that is grounded in day-to-day teaching practice and is designed to enhance teachers' content-specific instructional practices with the intent of improving student learning." Job-embedded professional development is different from traditional professional development offerings that often lack the necessary frequency and duration to prove effective in teacher development (Darling-Hammond, Hyler, & Gardner, 2017). Linda Darling-Hammond, Maria E. Hyler, and Madelyn Gardner (2017) encourage "moving away from traditional learning models that are generic and lecture based toward models that engage teachers directly in the practices they are learning and, preferably, are connected to teachers' classrooms and students." In his book *School Climate: Leading With Collective Efficacy*, author Peter M. DeWitt (2018) suggests job-embedded professional development offers the support needed for your teachers to believe in their teaching capabilities. Scholarly literature echoes this sentiment, pointing to a strong relationship between job-embedded professional development and the development of teacher self-efficacy (Althauser, 2015; Liu & Liao, 2019). If you want your teachers to develop self-efficacy, you need to provide them with practices that promote the use of mastery experiences.

In his book *Transforming Professional Development Into Student Results*, Douglas B. Reeves (2010) explains the type of effective professional development necessary to teach mastery experiences to your teachers by stating, "It is intensive and sustained, it is directly relevant to the needs of teachers and students, and it provides opportunities for application, practice, reflection, and reinforcement" (p. 23). These types of experiences give teachers the time to learn something new, try it out in their own setting, receive feedback, and make necessary adjustments to incrementally improve. For example, at the beginning of this chapter, we introduced you to Sarah, a second-grade teacher. Let's say one of Sarah's greatest first-year challenges was classroom management. To build Sarah's self-efficacy, or belief in her ability to successfully manage behaviors in her classroom, Sarah would need mastery experiences. Sarah's principal could have her observe teachers with effective classroom management techniques, practice those techniques in her own classroom, invite her mentor to participate in the practice sessions as an observer or co-teacher, and finally take time to reflect on the experience by receiving feedback from her mentor. The goal of this process would be for Sarah to feel confident in her abilities and reach a defined set of outcomes, no matter how long it takes to achieve.

Good instruction begins with a teacher's confidence in his or her abilities, knowing what good instruction looks like, and having some way to measure progress. In his book *Visible Learning for Teachers: Maximizing Impact on Learning*, John Hattie (2012) states:

> Two powerful ways of increasing impact are to know *and* share both the learning intentions and success criteria of the lesson with students. When students know both, they are more likely to work towards mastering the criteria of success, more likely to know where they are on the trajectory towards this success, and more likely to have a good chance of learning how to monitor and self-regulate their progress. (p. 67)

Susan Totaro and Mark Wise (2018) suggest applying Hattie's (2012) findings to teachers, helping them increase their instructional impact. Like students, teachers need to know expectations and action steps that will help them define whether or not they are successful. Harvard professors Rhonda Bondie and David Dockterman (2018) take this one step further by suggesting the use of a progress-monitoring tool for teachers to actively assess their growth. Teachers, coaches, mentors, or administrators can do progression monitoring; however, the person that keeps track of the progress is less important than the ongoing dialogue that should happen between the teacher and primary support person. Your school may choose to use its current teacher evaluation tool for defined teacher outcomes. If this is the case, we encourage you to develop action steps for success with your staff, determining actions your teachers can take that will help them get to the specific teacher outcome. We offer figure 2.2 as an example that identifies action steps from a teaching outcome and a tool for progress monitoring. You can use the "Job-Embedded Professional Development Tracker Template" reproducible at the end of the chapter (page 53) as a template as you develop job-embedded professional development plans with your teachers.

Teaching Outcome	Action Steps for Success	Progress Monitoring
The teacher will successfully manage classroom behaviors.	• A clear set of co-created classroom behavior expectations are posted in the classroom. • Students know what each behavior expectation looks like, sounds like, and feels like. • Teacher understanding of the classroom behavior expectations is evident as the teacher proactively addresses behavior concerns. • Classroom routines and procedures are evident.	**Date:** 10/1 **Comments:** There is evidence of classroom co-created behavior expectations posted in the classroom. Next to each expectation is a chart listing what each behavior looks like, sounds like, and feels like. **Next Steps:** Begin to work on addressing classroom behavior expectations in a proactive manner.

Source: Adapted from Bondie & Dockterman, 2018; Hattie, 2012.

Figure 2.2: Job-embedded professional development tracker example.

Job-embedded professional development should provide successful experiences for your teachers while simultaneously stretching them to new levels of teaching. Do not take this balance lightly. It's important to realize success without challenge and discomfort may not lead to further growth. However, repeated failure with no small victories *will not* lead to greater teacher self-efficacy (Bandura, 1994; Bjork & Bjork, 2011).

In addition, professional development can feel punitive when forced on your staff. You need to be crystal clear that you believe in your teachers and that you are providing these experiences so that they can develop their belief in themselves. Your teachers will take this to heart if you've established the relational precondition of trust. We encourage you to consider how your current professional development offerings yield mastery experiences for your teachers. The "Mastery Experience Considerations Template" reproducible at the end of the chapter (page 54) is a template for you as you consider implementing mastery experiences in your school.

INSIGHTS FROM THE FIELD

"Teaching is the hardest and most demanding profession in the world. Teachers are asked to meet the academic, physical, and social-emotional needs of each of their students. This takes a toll on a teacher's physical, mental, emotional, and spiritual strengths. As a leader, I believe empowering teachers is the oxygen in the blood that can sustain a teacher. As a leader, if I build a system that empowers teachers to be creative, risk-takers, and leaders, they will infuse those qualities into their students . . . through data and discussion, I can help a teacher see their impact. I believe that a teacher who knows they are effective will be more confident and empowered to do more for their students."

—Principal, personal communication, June 23, 2020

Create Self-Efficacious Working Conditions

The cornerstone of developing a teacher's self-efficacy is creating conditions that support what Bandura (1994) refers to as the physiological states of your teachers. When leaders focus on creating an environment that supports the emotions and moods of their teachers, they influence the feel of the environment, creating a sense of safety and well-being among their staff. Teachers are more likely to believe in their potential and capabilities when working in an environment where they feel safe enough to try new things knowing they may fail the first time around. In his book *Leaders Eat Last: Why Some Teams Pull Together and Others Don't*, thought leader Simon Sinek (2014) explains that providing safety is a primary catalyst for building a culture of trust and interdependence. He goes on to explain that if leaders want their employees to be happy and give their very best, they don't "set out to change their employees—they set out to change the conditions in which their employees operate" (Sinek, 2014, p. 15).

Research tells us self-efficacy development is dependent on a working environment that inhibits stress-making factors (Skaalvik & Skaalvik, 2016). Yet, things like punitive school accountability measures, such as providing sanctions for poor performances on test scores and deadlines for achieving set growth, are shown to elevate working conditions that create stress. In fact, teachers are more likely to leave their positions when consequences are tied to poor performance (Ingersoll, Merrill, & May, 2016).

Another condition amplifying stress within our schools is the state of our students' mental health and wellness. According to recent research, "Roughly half of American school children have experienced at least some form of trauma—from neglect, to abuse, to violence" (Lander, 2018). This means your teachers are on the front lines of supporting those students, and, in return, are feeling the effects of the students' trauma through secondary traumatic stress. The National Child Traumatic Stress Network (n.d.) defines secondary traumatic stress as "emotional duress that results when an individual hears about the firsthand trauma experiences of another." Essentially, your teachers begin their careers with a full gas tank of compassion. As they encounter student trauma after student trauma, they express compassion for their students, and their gas tank begins to empty. If your teachers get to the point where they completely empty their tank, they may exhibit signs such as:

> withdrawing from friends and family; feeling unexplainably irritable or angry or numb; inability to focus; blaming others; feeling hopeless or isolated or guilty about not doing enough; struggling to concentrate; being unable to sleep; overeating or not eating enough; and continually and persistently worrying about students, when they're at home and even in their sleep. (Lander, 2018)

Your teachers' tanks of compassion will need to be filled back up, or you'll have tired, stressed, burned-out teachers. One way to fill up their tanks is through the use of social persuasion.

In the following sections, we introduce you to two principals, Principal Carson and Principal Mayer. As you read through each scenario, look for the everyday practices they each exhibit. How does their use of language contribute to their work environments? What practices seem to build teachers' beliefs in themselves, and what practices destroy these beliefs? What is each principal doing or not doing to help teachers overcome even the most overwhelming circumstances?

Leadership Without Social Persuasion

As Principal Carson greets you at the entrance to the school building, you immediately notice her stoic demeanor. She explains to you that one of her newest teachers approached her that morning completely overwhelmed by her students' social-emotional needs. She questions whether her teacher has what it takes to meet the needs of all of these students. Principal Carson decides the best response is to give that teacher space and see how things play out. For Principal Carson, it's not a matter of *if* the stress and demands of teaching will cause this teacher to quit, it's a matter of *when*.

When you sit in on Principal Carson's morning staff meeting, one thing stands out: her ability to stick to her agenda like a pro. With state testing just around the corner, Principal Carson reminds her staff of the school community's expectations for great results. She goes on to share with her staff she has no control over such mandates and that the important thing is for them to just get through it. Principal Carson then transitions to staff acknowledgments, praising the whole staff so as not to play favorites with certain individuals. Her praise consists of a reminder of the staff's hard work and encouragement to not lose focus, especially during such an important time as state testing. Principal Carson feels that too much praise weakens her staff's motivation and causes them to settle for mediocre results, so she quickly moves from this agenda item. Principal Carson ends the meeting by telling her staff, "Hang in there, everyone. By our count in the office, we have thirty-seven more days until summer vacation."

Leadership With Social Persuasion

As Principal Mayer greets you at the entrance to the school building, you immediately notice he's had a tough start to the day. He explains the morning was a challenge as one of his newest teachers came to him completely overwhelmed by her students' social-emotional needs. He goes on to commend this teacher's incredible resilience and his belief in her ability to overcome such a tough situation. Principal Mayer decides the best response to the situation is to check in with that teacher later in the day and reinforce his belief in her ability to meet the school's high expectations in responding to diverse student needs. For Principal Mayer, it's not a matter of *if* this teacher will be great, it's a matter of *when*.

As you sit in on Principal Mayer's morning staff meeting, one thing stands out: his ability to take a stressful circumstance and make it positive. With state testing just around the corner, Principal Mayer acknowledges the fact that each staff member may be feeling stress and pressure in different ways over the days to come. He tells them that he is there for them and that he believes in them. He shares with his staff examples of previous times their school has taken difficult situations and made the most of them. Principal Mayer then transitions to honoring school-related and non-school-related staff achievements. He praises them with clarity, telling the staff exactly what it was that they achieved, knowing his praise models a culture of risk taking and growth. Principal Mayer ends the meeting with the same quote he uses to end every meeting: "Failure is the key to our school's success. I'll never be more proud of you than when you screw up and learn from it. Screwing up means you're trying, trying means you're taking risks, and taking risks means you're growing. So, get out there and fail."

A leader's words are powerful. You will move your teachers' self-efficacy needle if you authentically express your belief in their capabilities. Like Principal Mayer, when you are purposeful about the words you use, the self-efficacious working conditions in your school will improve. Table 2.1 (page 50) shares times when you may use social persuasion and examples of what you might say.

Table 2.1: How and When to Use Social Persuasion

When should I use social persuasion?	What should I say?
When giving teachers positive feedback	"I knew you could do . . . because . . ."
When giving teachers negative feedback	"You haven't achieved . . . yet. But, I believe you have what it takes to do . . . because I've seen you do . . . in the past."
When problem solving with a teacher	"The last problem we solved together was . . . and we had a positive result. I believe we will have a positive result this time as well."
After a teacher setback	"Let's look at this as a growth opportunity. Failing doesn't mean it's over; it just means we give this another try."
After a teacher victory	"You've reached your goal of . . . I knew you could do it."
When preparing a teacher for what's to come	"You have experienced . . . in the past and have persevered. I believe you will persevere here as well."

Reflection

Our "Developing Teacher Self-Efficacy Rating Scale" reproducible can be found at the end of the chapter (page 55). The rating scale will help you assess your current state of developing teacher self-efficacy, identify areas of strength and needs for improvement, and focus on your professional learning progress.

What About the Support Staff?

- Empower staff to use their talents, skills, and abilities that go well beyond their defined school roles. Ask them how they feel their talents could be useful in the school, and share your insight on this as well.

- Honor staff members' time by inviting them to meetings and events that would be meaningful to them. However, acknowledge not every meeting may be pertinent. If you're not sure when to invite them, ask them what they think.

- Support staff efforts by providing hands-on modeling and the right resources for them to succeed. Then, praise their successes.

Conclusion

This chapter encouraged you to look outside yourself and ask the question "Who are you?" by placing emphasis on the development of teacher self-efficacy. Developing your teachers' self-efficacy helps your teachers believe in themselves, so that they may begin to look outward and ask the question "Who are we?" as a staff. Your teachers will never be able to believe in the power of the entire school's collective capabilities without believing in themselves first. Creating a school culture that honors well-developed self-efficacy will prove to be a necessary step as you reinforce to your staff that the ultimate success of a school will always be about *their* collective contributions within the school.

You can help your teachers develop their self-efficacy through high-impact teacher induction, job-embedded professional development opportunities, and self-efficacious working conditions. These supports will have lasting effects on your teacher retention efforts, but more importantly, they will have lasting effects *within* your teachers as they believe in themselves and their capabilities long after you're gone.

Talk It Over: Reflection Guide for Discussions

Growing as a learner and leader takes thoughtful reflection. Interacting with this book's text and listening to the experiences of others will make you more fully aware of who you are as a leader and the steps you can take to grow. Thoughtful conversations take time and energy, but investing in each other through conversation will establish the support group you will need when the going gets tough.

1. **Introducing yourself to the topic:** What is your experience working with a teacher with a high sense of self-efficacy? How has this teacher's self-efficacy affected your relationship with them? How has their self-efficacy affected the culture of the school?

2. **Looking inward:** What leadership actions known to develop teacher self-efficacy come most naturally to you? Which leadership actions present the greatest challenge?

3. **Making connections:** Take a moment to interact with the following statement by highlighting, underlining, or writing in the margins. Jot down questions or connections that you have with the statement in your life, community, and world. Then, share out your thoughts.

"Empowering teachers is the oxygen in the blood that can sustain a teacher. As a leader, if I build a system that empowers teachers to be creative, risk-takers, and leaders, they will infuse those qualities into their students."

—Principal, personal communication, June 23, 2020

4. **Applying it in practice:** Growing as a leader takes steps of action. You can do that with confidence when you share openly with others, supporting one another in those steps. Reflect on the "Developing Teacher Self-Efficacy Rating Scale" (page 55). Where is your greatest need for growth? What step will you take to grow in that area?

Job-Embedded Professional Development Tracker Template

Teaching Outcome	Action Steps for Success	Progress Monitoring
		Date: Comments: Next Steps:

Sources: Adapted from Bondie, R., & Dockterman, D. (2018). What strategy is most useful in promoting self-efficacy in educators and in learners? *Accessed at https://researchmap.digitalpromise.org /ask_a_researcher/ strategy-useful-promoting-self-efficacy-educators-learners/ on March 2, 2021; Hattie, J. (2012).* Visible learning for teachers: Maximizing impact on learning. *London: Routledge.*

Mastery Experience Considerations Template

Mastery Experience Considerations	Notes
Practice. What mastery experience does the teacher need?	
Frequency. How often does the teacher need supported experiences to develop the teaching practice?	
Duration. How long does the teacher need supported experiences to develop the teaching practice?	
Setting. When and where will the mastery experiences take place?	
Reflection. How will reflection be a part of the mastery experiences?	
Action steps for success. How will success be measured? How will teachers know what success is?	
Track progress. How will the teachers monitor their progress?	
Who. Who will act as the primary support person during the mastery experiences (coach, mentor, principal, for example)?	

Developing Teacher Self-Efficacy Rating Scale

Read each statement and reflect on how you rate in developing teacher self-efficacy. Then, determine next steps for growth.

Providing High-Impact Teacher Induction	Strongly Disagree	Somewhat Disagree	Somewhat Agree	Strongly Agree
I provide an orientation session to introduce new staff to the building.				
Next Steps:				
I pair new teachers with a mentor teacher who will act as their primary vicarious role model.				
Next Steps:				
I strategically place new teachers in a professional learning community for additional support.				
Next Steps:				
I give new teachers a chance to observe other teachers doing great work.				
Next Steps:				

Implementing Job-Embedded Professional Development	Strongly Disagree	Somewhat Disagree	Somewhat Agree	Strongly Agree
I use job-embedded professional development for my teachers to learn, practice, and reflect on their teaching.				
Next Steps:				
When teachers participate in job-embedded professional development, they have a primary support person coaching them along the way.				
Next Steps:				
I provide my teachers action steps toward teaching success and opportunities for progress.				
Next Steps:				
I am mindful of the words I use with teachers and how they contribute to the working environment.				
Next Steps:				

Creating Self-Efficacious Working Conditions	Strongly Disagree	Somewhat Disagree	Somewhat Agree	Strongly Agree
I acknowledge when teachers may be stressed or anxious.				
Next Steps:				
I share stories with teachers reminding them of times they overcame difficult circumstances or setbacks.				
Next Steps:				
My feedback to teachers is specific and clear.				
Next Steps:				
I communicate my belief in my teachers' capabilities.				
Next Steps:				

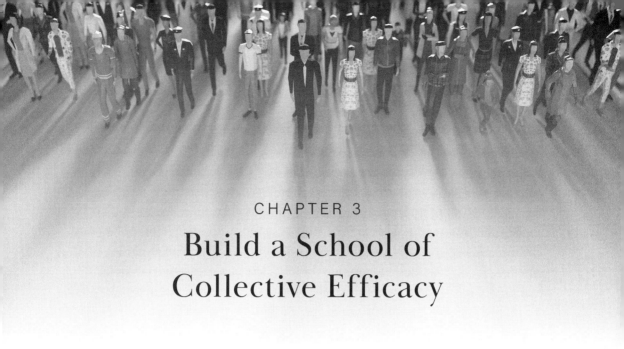

CHAPTER 3

Build a School of Collective Efficacy

*Interdependence is and ought to be as much
the ideal of man as self-sufficiency.*

—Gandhi

Aaron walked into Morris Middle School uncertain of what would lie before him, wondering if this would possibly be just another abbreviated stopover in a career full of moves. It was his third school in as many years, and he knew the reputation that preceded him. He was the dissatisfied teacher, the one that kept to himself, and the one that would jump ship at a moment's notice. Fifteen years before, Aaron entered the teaching profession with an optimistic outlook and a desire to be a part of something bigger than himself, but Aaron quickly realized bringing his strengths to the group was something his colleagues neither wanted nor needed. In fact, this couldn't have been more evident for Aaron when a colleague offered him some advice: "Keep your head down, close your door, and take care of your own classroom."

Aaron had transitioned from school to school during his career, looking for a place that felt like home. Through the years, a few lingering questions remained in his mind. Wasn't teaching supposed to be about serving the greater good? What would happen if teachers combined their individual talents by uniting as one to make a greater impact? He knew this was possible in his own classroom. Year after year, he would bring together a group of individual students under one common cause, helping them to believe in the power of the whole class and see that their differences truly made their classroom stronger. In the fifteen years of Aaron's career, he longed to be part of a school with teachers united under a common goal. Yet, he hadn't found that in a school, and he was quite certain schools like that didn't even exist. That is, until he walked into Morris Middle School.

When Aaron entered his first Morris Middle School staff meeting, he immediately knew things would be different. To his right was a large screen displaying a countdown to the start of the meeting. Next to the screen were a set of speakers playing inspirational music. To his left were several tables and chairs. One facilitator stood by each table, ready to welcome the teachers that were assigned to their table. As Aaron approached his assigned table, he noticed a signup sheet placed in the middle. The sheet had two columns, one for teachers willing to open their classroom to other teachers for observation opportunities and the other for those doing the observing. The meeting began with a group of teachers leading the staff in an article on building trust among colleagues. It continued with a data dive of all students grades 6 to 8 and a discussion on meeting the unique needs of several specific students. It ended with a listening session as the principal opened the floor for staff to share their voices.

While participating in his first staff meeting, three things came to Aaron's mind. First, it was apparent that each teacher was using their own strengths to help the staff. Each person had a role, and because of this, there was a sense of interdependence among them. Second, an underlying theme of the entire meeting was *learning together*. No matter the task, the staff seemed to believe they could accomplish it, and because of this, there was a strong sense of collaboration among them. Third, a school like this takes a concentrated effort and a selfless leader. No matter the agenda item, very rarely did it seem like one person was in charge; school leaders were not afraid to share ownership of ideas and gave staff members opportunities to lead.

As the school year progressed, Aaron knew he wasn't going to find another school like this one. A school with a culture built on interdependence and collaboration, where the uniqueness of each individual shined not for themselves but for everyone else. A school that believed that together they could make a difference, together they were better. This was *more* than a school. This school became Aaron's second family and was a place he called home for the remainder of his career.

Have you ever been inside a school like Aaron's? A school so special that it could only be described as magical? Why do some schools have *it* while others don't? Why do some schools consistently keep their teachers while others have what teacher retention experts Richard Ingersoll and Henry May (2016) call a "revolving door" (p. 4) of teachers? To understand the answers to these questions, it's time to look at whether or not your teachers believe in their collective capability. It's time to look at their collective efficacy.

In this chapter, we discuss what collective efficacy is and why it matters before discovering several strategies on how you as a leader can build collective efficacy. You will then have the opportunity to assess how you currently build collective efficacy and reflect on the impact of your leadership on the wider school community.

What Is Collective Efficacy?

Lasting leadership within a group is built and maintained through the collective beliefs of that group. In this chapter, we focus on the third ripple of our Lasting Legacy model—the question Who are we? (see figure 3.1). The answer to this question will unite your staff and will act as the foundation for whether or not your staff will believe in their collective capabilities. Your teachers' beliefs in each other will guide their actions and allow them to openly share, discuss, and collectively grow as a group. That is why you can't ignore building collective efficacy within your staff.

Figure 3.1: The third ripple in the Lasting Legacy model.

Albert Bandura (1998) broadens the concept of self-efficacy to encompass the collective. He describes collective efficacy as "people's shared beliefs in their collective power to produce desired outcomes" (p. 65). When your staff have a strong sense of collective efficacy, it will directly shape:

> the types of futures [your teachers] seek to achieve through collective action, how well they use their resources, how much effort they put into their group endeavor, their staying power when collective efforts fail to produce quick results or meet forcible opposition, and their vulnerability to the discouragement that can beset people taking on tough social problems. (Bandura, 2000, p. 75)

Collective efficacy is much like self-efficacy in that the same sources that develop individual teacher self-efficacy also develop collective efficacy. In the following list, we offer each of Bandura's (1994) four sources of efficacy that we presented in the previous chapter. Here, these sources are positioned within the context of a whole school.

1. **Mastery experiences:** Mastery experiences provide opportunities for your staff to experience success as a whole. You need to give your staff the chance to set realistic collective goals, work toward those goals, and

accomplish the goals together. Your staff will believe in their collective capabilities when they experience challenging circumstances and rely on one another to overcome challenges as a group.

2. **Vicarious experiences:** For your staff to believe in their collective capabilities, they need to see others like them perform tasks similar to the tasks they face. You can do this by giving your staff chances to observe and learn from one another, go on site visits to other schools, or watch others perform tasks through multimedia tools.

3. **Social persuasion:** Much like an individual teacher does, your staff need to hear they have what it takes to accomplish a goal. You will influence their collective belief when you choose your words purposefully. Your staff will only believe in their collective capabilities when *you* believe in their collective capabilities and develop the appropriate conditions for belief to happen. Social persuasion will influence your staff's collective efficacy when collaboration and communication become the norm throughout the school (Loughland & Ryan, 2020).

4. **Physiological state:** Your staff's collective ability to respond to stressful situations will either amplify or diminish their collective efficacy. Your charge as leader is to help your staff navigate through challenging situations so that they feel more confident in their collective capability the next time they face a similar challenge.

While much of Bandura's initial work on the sources of efficacy dates back to the 1970s, many of his concepts are embedded within today's most effective school processes, frameworks, and systems. Take, for instance, the professional learning community process. Bandura's (1994) four sources of efficacy are interwoven throughout the elements that make professional learning communities effective. Essentially, professional learning communities act as the vehicle for providing mastery learning experiences for your staff. As your staff work toward accomplishing a set of action steps and goals, they vicariously learn from one another, seeing and experiencing great teaching in action (DuFour et al., 2016). Furthermore, high-functioning professional learning communities follow established norms and protocols, creating environments that support what Bandura (1994) refers to as the physiological state of your teachers. Finally, professional learning communities tap into Bandura's source of social persuasion as they routinely see and hear their accomplishments through celebrations.

Why Does Collective Efficacy Matter?

Your teachers need to work in an environment where they have the ability to say, "I don't have to do this alone." Making a difference in the lives of students is not the responsibility of one teacher; it is the responsibility of the entire staff. Building a school of collective efficacy will create the conditions necessary to retain your teachers and instill a lasting belief *in each other*. Research suggests teachers are more committed and more likely to stay in their school when they feel they are a part of a school team that can successfully make a difference together (Donohoo, 2018). This is important considering the high turnover rates in high-poverty schools, where students face overwhelming external influences that affect how they perform. Keeping teachers in high-poverty schools is one of the greatest teacher retention challenges. In some ways, the socioeconomic status of students predicts whether or not teachers will stay in their buildings. Teacher retention is also a strong predictor of student achievement. Yet, Nicole S. Simon and Susan Moore Johnson (2015) suggest teachers in high-poverty schools don't leave their schools because of the challenges the students bring to the school; rather, they leave because of the lack of conditions known to promote collective efficacy. Simon and Johnson (2015) state:

> Teachers who leave high-poverty schools are not fleeing their students. Rather, they are fleeing the poor working conditions that make it difficult for them to teach and for their students to learn. The working conditions that teachers prize most—and those that best predict their satisfaction and retention—are social in nature. They include school leadership, collegial relationships, and elements of school culture. (p. 1)

Your teachers' belief in their collective capability is one of only a few factors that outweigh the impact of socioeconomic status on student achievement (Hoy, Tarter, & Hoy, 2006). In his seminal research of more than 1,500 meta-analyses, John Hattie identifies teacher collective efficacy as the single most determining factor in student achievement (Visible Learning, 2021). When teachers believe in their collective capabilities, they stay in their schools (Donohoo, 2018). When teachers stay in their schools, they build a belief in their capacity to accomplish challenges as a group, which elevates the outcomes of their students (Donohoo, Hattie, & Eells, 2018).

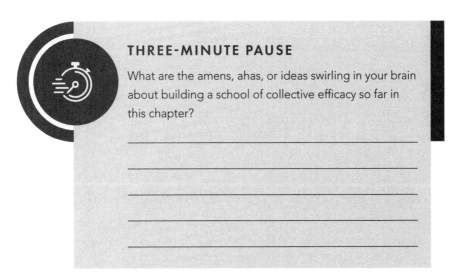

THREE-MINUTE PAUSE

What are the amens, ahas, or ideas swirling in your brain about building a school of collective efficacy so far in this chapter?

How Do I Build Collective Efficacy?

Building collective efficacy is often like building a campfire. We start with a stack of wood, or a set of individuals each with a different purpose and a different role essential to the creation and sustainability of the fire. We begin the fire with kindling—a core group of teacher leaders believing in the power of one another. We give the kindling a spark, igniting a flame with the necessary conditions, words, and supports to grow the belief. The flame will spread easily with some while it will take time, patience, and the right environment for others. As the fire grows, more individuals will ignite and begin to believe in the power of one another. The lit wood will serve as the visible foundation—those who stand out to us—providing light and warmth to those around them in hopes to catch fire to those that have not been lit. As leaders, we keep the fire going by fueling it with the unique talents of our people. We tend the fire with those talents, feeding our schools with their gifts when the opportunities arise. Each piece of firewood offers its own unique contribution toward the development of one single, powerful flame. Our job as leaders is to monitor the conditions surrounding the fire, knowing the right conditions play a role in its growth and sustainability. Ultimately, our goal is to shine our light as one united school to even the darkest of places.

A strong sense of collective efficacy in your school will unquestionably influence the outcomes of your teachers and students. So, what are you intentionally doing to build the collective efficacy within your school? Are you creating an environment where your teachers feel they are a part of something bigger than themselves? Are you providing a spark that will ignite your teachers' belief in their collective capabilities? Do you know what it will take to build their collective efficacy? The remainder of this chapter discusses three ways to build the collective efficacy of your staff: (1) build shared leadership, (2) create collective learning opportunities, and (3) create a positive school climate through social support.

Build Shared Leadership

Your staff will never believe in their collective capacity unless you give them a chance to share their gifts with one another. For this reason, building shared leadership throughout your school is essential. Research suggests shared leadership strongly relates to the collective efficacy beliefs of your teachers. Collective efficacy increases among school staff when principals believe all teachers have what it takes to lead (Derrington & Angelle, 2013). In his book *In Praise of American Educators*, Richard DuFour (2015) further explains the critical need for educational leaders to share their leadership by saying:

> No one person has the energy, expertise, and influence to fulfill all of the responsibilities of your job successfully. If you try to do it all by yourself,

you will fail. The only hope of meeting the demands of the contempo-
rary principalship is dispersing leadership throughout the school. (p. 225)

Sharing leadership with your staff will highlight the contributions each staff member
can bring to the school, a necessary ingredient for your staff to realize the power of
the whole school rather than the power of one administrator. To build shared leadership among your staff, you need to know your teachers not just as employees but as
people with talents, skills, and abilities to be shared. We encourage you to ask yourself, "Do I truly know who my teachers are?" and "Do I know them to the point
where I could name each of their strengths?" Better yet, if one of your teachers asked
you, could you answer the following questions?

- Do you know what I'm passionate about?

- Do you know what I want to be involved in?

- Do you know what I'm good at?

If you can answer these questions, you are well on your way to aligning individuals with leadership opportunities that tap into who they are as people and the talents,
skills, and abilities they possess. What do you do if you don't know these answers?
How can you begin to understand the strengths and passions of your teachers, and
how can you align those to leadership opportunities in your school?

We often encourage leaders to start by having each member of their staff take a personality inventory or survey that helps them determine their unique strengths. Finding
the right personality inventory or survey for you and your staff will depend on several
variables. You'll want to consider your available resources, the amount of time you have
for your staff to take the inventory or survey, the number of staff within your school
community, how you will deliver the inventory or survey, how you plan to collect
and analyze the data, and your goal or purpose for using the survey. As you're trying
to determine the most appropriate personality inventory or survey, you may want to
pilot one with a leadership, grade-level, or subject-area team to see if it will meet your
school's needs. Regardless of the inventory or survey you choose, your ultimate goal
should always be to choose one that will help you better understand your staff. After
survey completion, a few principals we know have charted their staff's strengths on a
matrix, allowing them to easily identify how the strengths among the staff are alike
and different. Using a matrix can also act as a quick reference for you when looking
for certain strengths that align with shared leadership opportunities that arise in the
school. For example, perhaps the personality inventory you used with your staff identified certain staff members with the strength of relating to others. You could use the
matrix to help determine individuals that may want to be greeters for an open house.
Figure 3.2 (page 66) shows an example matrix listing the names of staff members
in a building and their strengths that were identified through a personality inventory. As new staff enter your building, the personality inventory or survey can serve

	Flexible	Leadership	Decisive	Teamwork	Relational
Mr. Bobb	X				X
Ms. Jensen		X	X	X	X
Mrs. Brown	X			X	X
Mr. Nelson		X	X		
Mr. Dee		X		X	

Figure 3.2: Sample matrix for personality inventory or survey.

as onboarding for you and these individuals. At this time, you can acknowledge your new staff's strengths and the great attributes they are bringing to your building well before their school year even begins. Then, have your staff complete the "Strengths and Passions Reflection Tool" found at the end of the chapter (page 76). Collecting the responses from this tool will help further your understanding of each staff member's strengths, passions, and areas they would like to be involved in.

Once you know the strengths and passions of your teachers, then we recommend you humbly get out of the way. Sharing leadership with your staff does not mean you are less capable of leading, but it does mean you actually have to let your staff lead. Principals who share leadership with their staff provide both choice and voice to their teachers' leadership opportunities.

Many teachers can share a time when their principal completely disregarded their own professional discretion and placed them on a committee or in a leadership role without their input. For shared leadership to increase collective efficacy in your school, your teachers need to have a choice in *how* they lead (Angelle & Teague, 2014). For example, one high school principal gave choice by providing a detailed list of school leadership opportunities with descriptions to the staff, allowing staff members to choose their preference. This list included opportunities such as the building leadership team, technology committee, or response-to-intervention team. Staff members were asked to choose one leadership opportunity to participate in that aligned with their personal strengths and passions. You will find some of your teachers will steer toward leadership opportunities that highlight their personal strengths while others will feel compelled to offer their leadership in areas they are passionate about. Perhaps more service-oriented teachers will desire to be a part of leadership opportunities that center on giving back to the community. Others that are more task-oriented may align with leadership opportunities such as data-driven decision making. Whatever their strengths or passions, giving your teachers choice in the matter will dramatically increase their investment and involvement.

Once you've given your staff a choice in shared leadership, then you need to allow them to lead by actually giving them a voice in decision making. In his book

School Climate: Leading With Collective Efficacy, Peter M. DeWitt (2018) emphasizes the critical relationship between developing teacher efficacy and giving teachers a voice. He says, "We should no longer be taking away the decision-making power of teachers because we begin to enable them and not empower them" (DeWitt, 2018, p. 100). Principals who take the time to listen empower their teachers to stand up and lead when the moment is right. A principal we've worked with reminded us that allowing our staff to be a part of the decision-making process can increase their sense of autonomy and ownership in the school. Principal Samson encourages leaders to give a voice to their teachers by trusting in their leadership capabilities and by remaining compassionate. While sharing leadership is not always easy, he explains the rewards that come with it by saying, "Open, honest dialogue takes time, but the fruits of those labors will surely be a better classroom, school, and district in its entirety" (W. Samson, personal communication, July 10, 2020).

INSIGHTS FROM THE FIELD

"I have learned to promote authentic collaboration, dialogue, and trust among groups. Teachers need to feel free to express their views. The language school leaders use influences how teachers view themselves within the learning community. As curriculum coordinator, I engage in a lot of conversations with teachers as each grade level plans, analyzes data, and reflects on teaching and learning. I am mindful of the questions I ask and how I ask questions so that my questions encourage meaningful professional dialogue. School leaders need to establish essential agreements that encourage teachers to voice their opinions, critique, and self-assess respectfully and express any confusion. Professional discussion is critical for nurturing relationships and building a culture of collaboration among teachers."

—Curriculum coordinator,
personal communication, July 19, 2020

Create Collective Learning Opportunities

A vital key to building collective efficacy in your school is providing experiences for your teachers to learn and grow together in a safe, encouraging, and supportive environment. For you, this means developing a process that encompasses all four sources of collective efficacy: (1) mastery experiences, (2) vicarious experiences, (3) social persuasion, and (4) physiological state. As a principal, one of this book's authors, Becky, and colleague Crystal Hintzman, developed a process to support their staff's collective growth and belief in each other. Figure 3.3 shows the progression of this model.

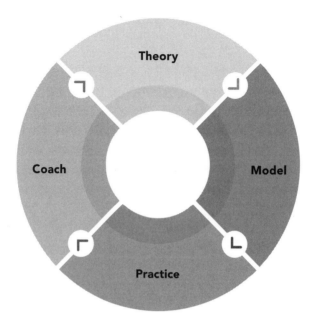

Figure 3.3: Theory, model, practice, coach process.

The four parts of this process are (1) theory, (2) model, (3) practice, and (4) coach. The following sections will detail how to complete each part of this process.

Theory

When looking at this model, the first step is to determine your staff's collective efficacy needs and the theory, or scholarly research, that supports the development of that need. Ask yourself, "What is the knowledge, skill, or disposition we need as a staff to further develop our belief in each other?" We encourage you to use your leadership team to discuss what those needs may be by asking the following questions.

- "What do we try to achieve together in our school, and what do we try to achieve alone?"

- "In what areas do we work the hardest as a group, and in what areas do we not?"

- "In what areas do we persevere as a group, and in what areas do we not?"

The answers to these questions will help define the areas where your staff have a collective belief in each other and the areas in need of development. Every staff will have unique collective efficacy developmental needs. For example, some schools will need to focus on student discipline and behavior management, while others will need to focus on communicating with families. Whatever the area of need, you want your staff to believe they are better unified than alone.

Becky's leadership team determined it needed to develop as a whole staff in the area of classroom instruction. Specifically, the team recognized inconsistencies throughout the school in providing clear learning targets to students. Some teachers created and used learning targets on their own, while others did not use them at all. Because of this, the leadership team knew it needed to provide the necessary conditions for the staff to implement learning targets in every classroom *together*. Figure 3.4 is an example of communication from Becky's leadership team to her staff.

To: Staff
From: Building Leadership Team
Subject: This Year's Teaching Strategy Focus

As a leadership team, we want to share with you that what you do in the classroom makes a difference. However, we have limited time with our students, and we want to focus on the strategies that will have the greatest positive impact for our students and will help our staff unite under one common purpose.

The strategy that we have chosen to focus on this year for our school-improvement plan is developing our clarity as teachers by providing clear learning targets to our students. Our work *together* will make a difference in the lives of our kids!

In John Hattie's (2012) book *Visible Learning for Teachers*, he has researched strategies that have the greatest positive impact on students. John Hattie followed a meta-analysis, a recognized statistical procedure, that allowed researchers to combine the data from many studies on a particular topic to understand the impact on student learning. His original work actually had 800 meta-analyses that combined 50,000 individual studies involving 250 million students. From this work, he was able to see the real effect of the strategy being implemented.

The effect size of teacher clarity, a part of which is providing clear learning targets to students, is 0.75 on a 1.00 scale (Hattie, 2012). With an effect size of 0.75, it can double the gains in student learning. That means a struggling student, lagging a year behind his peers in reading, can make double the gains in a year of instruction.

Source: Copyright © 2013 by Piedmont Elementary School, Duluth, Minnesota. Used with permission.

Figure 3.4: Building leadership team letter to staff.

When you and your leadership team have chosen a collective efficacy area of need, guide your staff through the theory behind your decision. Theory will give your staff the *why* behind what you are doing as a staff. For instance, Becky's staff built shared knowledge with regard to providing clear learning targets to students by reviewing relevant literature together, listening to podcasts, and connecting with others in the field.

Model

The second step is to model addressing the chosen area of need for your staff so they can see the behaviors entailed in successfully meeting the need. This is akin to what Bandura (1994) calls *vicarious experiences*. Your staff need ample opportunities to learn from one another in a safe format. Becky's leadership team used two methods to model its strategy to staff. The first was a mock team meeting, modeling how a team could develop learning targets based on the grade-level standards and how to state those learning targets in student-friendly terms. The second was a mock classroom observation experience demonstrating how the use of learning targets could be integrated into classroom instruction. Staff were given an observational checklist and asked to look for teacher and student evidence of clearly provided learning targets. The "Staff Observational Checklist" reproducible found at the end of the chapter (page 77) is an example of such a checklist.

Practice

The third step in creating a collective learning opportunity for your staff is to set aside time to practice. The purpose of this step is two-fold. First, it gives teachers mastery learning experiences as they learn and work on something new together. As your teachers participate in a successful practice experience as a group, they will use that success to believe in their collective capability. The second purpose is to increase the positive physiological state of your staff. Practice sessions help alleviate stress and anxiety by allowing your teachers to work together, ask questions, and address any challenges they have prior to performing the task in their own classrooms. We recommend that you have your leadership team available to answer questions, provide feedback, and acknowledge the efforts of the staff. For Becky's staff, they partnered up and practiced walking through the observational checklist with a colleague.

Coach

Peer coaching is the fourth and final step in creating a collective learning opportunity for your staff. At this point, your staff have learned, observed, and practiced a desired task. Now, it's time for them to implement what they've learned into their own setting using peer coaching. *Peer coaching* refers to two teachers taking turns observing each other teaching (Knight et al., 2015). One will teach while the other will observe. A primary component to this step is the use of social persuasion among your staff. You'll want your staff to use a staff observational checklist (see page 77) or a peer coaching form (see page 78). These tools will help elevate the conditions for social persuasion by promoting open, honest communication, and collaboration.

Peer coaching also promotes two other sources of collective efficacy. First, those doing the observing will experience vicarious learning by watching their colleague perform a task that they themselves will eventually perform. Second, colleague observation, rather than administrator observation, is less threatening when teachers are initially implementing a new strategy in their classroom, and less perceived threat supports the physiological state of your teachers. The "Peer Coaching Pre- and Post-Observation Conference Worksheet" found at the end of the chapter (page 79) is an example of a peer coaching observation form that can guide your staff through reflection before and after the observation.

A question we often hear is, "How do you find time and resources for your teachers to observe one another?" Becky, her school social worker, and the instructional coach set up a schedule where they were available to come into their teachers' classrooms and fill in while they performed a peer observation. They always planned for enough time for pre-observation discussion, observation, and a follow-up reflection session to occur.

Ultimately, the goal of creating collective learning opportunities is to develop the collective efficacy in your staff. Collective efficacy increases when your teachers authentically collaborate, learn from one another, and rely on each other for their professional growth (Donohoo et al., 2018). By following the four-step process of theory, model, practice, and coach, you will be giving your staff a chance to learn and grow together in a way that incorporates each one of Bandura's (1994) sources of collective efficacy.

Create a Positive School Climate

While the preceding collective-efficacy-building strategies will prove essential to your staff's belief in their capabilities as a whole, they may induce stress or anxiety if you don't consider the conditions you are creating. Building collective efficacy will not happen without creating the conditions that also build a positive school climate.

Leading school climate researcher Wayne K. Hoy (1990) defines school climate as "the relatively enduring quality of the school environment that is experienced by participants, affects their behavior, and is based on their collective perceptions of behavior in school" (p. 152). The National School Climate Council (as cited in Thapa, Cohen, Guffey, & Higgins-D'Alessandro, 2013) adds to this definition by explaining school climate as the "patterns of people's experiences of school life and reflects norms, goals, values, interpersonal relationships, teaching and learning practices, and organizational structures" (p. 358). Essentially, how the atmosphere in your school *feels* to your teachers will directly influence their day-to-day experiences. Together your teachers navigate what they want to achieve, what they deem acceptable among each other, what they collectively believe in, the quality of their relationships, and how safe they feel (Thapa et al., 2013). If your teachers perceive their school climate as positive, they will be more likely to stay in their positions (Dahlkamp, Peters, & Schumacher, 2017). However, if they perceive the school climate as one that provokes stress and anxiety, they will leave (Clement, 2017).

The social relationships within your school will largely influence your school's climate and ultimately your staff's collective efficacy (Avanzi, Schuh, Fraccaroli, & van Dick, 2015). That's why social support within your school is foundational to how your teachers *feel* in the school. *Social support* is generally defined as individuals' feeling that others care for and value them for who they are (Liu, Gou, & Zuo, 2016). In the context of the school, social support is typically provided by teacher colleagues, staff, and administration. Research suggests social support is critical to improving mental health and well-being and can help individuals combat stress (Camara, Bacigalupe, & Padilla, 2017). In his model of social support, Charles Tardy suggests four areas where social support can be provided: (1) emotional, (2) informational, (3) instrumental, and (4) appraisal support (as cited in Demaray, Malecki, Secord, & Lyell, 2012). Using this model of social support, the following is an example of how one principal helped build collective efficacy in his staff by influencing the school climate through social support.

With finals just around the corner, Principal Carry's staff are feeling overwhelmed, stressed, and unsure of how prepared their students will be. Recognizing the tense atmosphere in the school, Principal Carry chooses to emotionally support his staff by sending the following message:

> May 17
>
> Hey folks! With finals just around the corner I sense some warranted stress coming from our classrooms. I just wanted to let you know I'm here for you, I believe in you, and I know you can persevere during this difficult time. I encourage you to lean on each other and swing into my office to chat about questions or concerns—I'd be happy to listen! Remember, we're all in this together!

After emailing the staff, Principal Carry prepares a small flier to be distributed in teacher mailboxes. The flier includes facts and statistics about ways to cope during times of stress, a type of informational support for his staff. Knowing his teachers could realistically use the time to plan and prepare for finals, he then proceeds to cancel the next day's after-school technology training, showing his instrumental support. Finally, Principal Carry supports his staff through appraisal by creating a list of five characteristics the staff possess that can help them persevere together. He adds this list of praise to the school's daily staff bulletin.

While this may be a simple example of how one principal provides support for his staff, it illustrates the approach principals can take when their staff's physiological state is in question. There are certain times during the school year that can be more stressful for your staff than others. It may be necessary to pull back on professional development trainings, initiatives, or excess staff meetings during these times. You can map out these times on a school calendar with a team of teacher leaders to identify the points in the year when you may need to take a pause and allow your teachers to focus on the task at hand (for example, conferences, an open house, or state assessments). Additionally, if you want social support to increase among your staff, they will need to spend quality time together, learning one another's beliefs and values. While sometimes overlooked, community-building activities can prove essential in creating a positive school climate. Table 3.1 (page 74) provides a list of activities you can use to deepen the relationships in your school and help your teachers learn about each other to a greater extent.

Reflection

You will find our "Building a School of Collective Efficacy Rating Scale" at the end of the chapter (page 80). The rating scale will help you assess your current state of building a school of collective efficacy, identify areas of strength and needs for improvement, and provide focus to your professional learning progress.

What About the Support Staff?

- Plan team-building exercises throughout the year that include your support staff, giving them a chance to experience success with others throughout the building.

- Include staff when problem solving as a team. Seek their advice and consider their input.

- Provide shared leadership opportunities in the building, allowing staff members to serve as representatives on committees, including them, and listening to their perspectives.

Conclusion

Staff who look beyond themselves ask the question "Who are we?" and build collective efficacy. Developing collective efficacy within your school will prove to be an important component to retaining your teachers and leaving a lasting legacy. In their book *You Win in the Locker Room First*, Jon Gordon and Mike Smith (2015) explain what can happen when your staff begin to believe in their collective capabilities by saying:

> If we stayed together and battled through the ups and downs of the season and continually worked on staying connected…we were always going to be in a position to get the outcome that we wanted. We knew that when it was time for someone to step up and make a game-changing play, that we would get it done. When your team is connected, you have the synergy within the organization that will not allow your team to disintegrate. (p. 74)

Table 3.1: Activities for Laughter and Fun

Activity	Description
Spin the Wheel	Staff spin the wheel when they reach a goal or complete a task. On the wheel is a list of fun, affordable prizes, which are changed on a regular basis. As one example, a staff member may get to borrow the principal's chair for a day.
Crazy Friday	Staff and students can wear something fun and different to work—for example, their favorite hat or bedroom slippers.
Hula Hoop Contest	Staff members battle by grade level or department to see who can hula-hoop the longest.
Popcorn Friday	Pop popcorn on Friday for the staff to have with their lunch.
Golf Putting Contest in the Hallway	Have all of the staff begin with a ten-foot putt. Those who successfully hole the ten-foot putt will move on to a thirty-foot putt. Those who hole the thirty-foot putt will then move on to a final fifty-foot (or longer!) putt for the grand prize.
T-ball Game	Set up a T-ball game where the students battle the staff.
Staff Potluck	Have staff bring their favorite dish to share with their colleagues.
Candy Welcome	Greet staff at the entrance as they come in and thank them for coming to work. Give them some Life Savers or another type of candy that fits the occasion.
Human Bowling	Use two-liter soda bottles for the pins. The bowling ball is a staff member sitting on two scooters tied together horizontally. Then another staff member bowls by rolling or pushing the scooter down the bowling lane to see how many pins as a team they can knock down.
Good News Phone Calls	The building leader calls a significant person in the teacher's life to share how the teacher is appreciated at the school.
Secret Pals	Host a secret-pals week within your building. Staff members are randomly assigned a person for whom they do acts of kindness during the week without the staff member knowing their identity. Then at the end of the week the secret pals reveal themselves.
Just-for-Fun Bulletin Board	Post white bulletin board paper in the hallway and let students and staff contribute whatever they want—just for fun!
Book Exchange	Encourage staff to share and exchange books that they are reading for professional learning and enjoyment during a staff meeting.

Building collective efficacy in your school will equip your staff to weather the ups and downs of their school year, remain committed to their collective goals, and build a *belief in each other* that informs an understanding that they can accomplish anything together even when you, their leader, are gone. You will ignite their beliefs in the collective whole by providing shared leadership, creating collective learning opportunities, and creating a positive school climate.

Talk It Over: Reflection Guide for Discussions

Growing as a learner and leader takes thoughtful reflection. Interacting with this book's text and listening to the experiences of others will make you more fully aware of who you are as a leader and the steps you can take to grow. Thoughtful conversations take time and energy, but investing in each other through conversation will establish the support group you will need when the going gets tough.

1. **Introducing yourself to the topic:** What is your experience working in a school or on a committee or task force with a high sense of collective efficacy? Why do you think there was a high sense of collective efficacy?

2. **Looking inward:** Building collective efficacy calls for finding common ground among others and tapping into the unique gifts of individuals. Is it easier for you personally to help your staff find common ground or for you to notice the unique differences among your staff? Why do you think that is?

3. **Making connections:** Take a moment to interact with the following statement by highlighting, underlining, or writing in the margins. Jot down questions or connections that you have with the statement in your life, community, and world. Then, share out your thoughts.

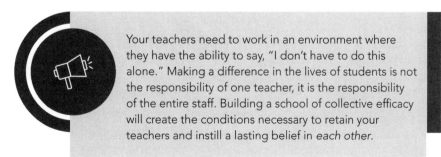

Your teachers need to work in an environment where they have the ability to say, "I don't have to do this alone." Making a difference in the lives of students is not the responsibility of one teacher, it is the responsibility of the entire staff. Building a school of collective efficacy will create the conditions necessary to retain your teachers and instill a lasting belief in *each other*.

4. **Applying it in practice:** Growing as a leader takes steps of action. You can take the steps with confidence when you share openly with others, supporting one another in those steps. Reflect on the "Building a School of Collective Efficacy Rating Scale" (page 80). Where is your greatest need for growth? What step will you take to grow in that area?

Strengths and Passions Reflection Tool

According to the personality inventory, what are your three greatest strengths?	1. 2. 3.
What are the three things you are most passionate about at our school?	1. 2. 3.
When considering your strengths and passions, what are three things you would like to be involved in at our school?	1. 2. 3.

Staff Observational Checklist

Providing Clear Learning Targets			
Goal: The teacher provides a clearly stated **learning target**.			
Teacher Evidence		**Student Evidence**	
	The **learning target** is stated in student-friendly terms.		When asked, students can explain the **learning target** for the lesson.
	The **learning target** is posted in the same spot each day.		
	The **learning target** is stated verbally.		When asked, students can explain how their current activity relates to the **learning target**.
	Teacher calls attention to the **learning target** during the lesson.		
	Teacher summarizes the **learning target** at the end of the lesson.		

Notes:

Source: Copyright © 2013 by Piedmont Elementary School, Duluth, Minnesota. Used with permission.

Peer Coaching Form

Date:

Focus of Lesson:

I Saw	I Heard	I Observed
Example: You displayed a copy of the student workbook page on the SMART Board.	Example: "Here are the key learning targets for today . . ."	Example: Most students were following along during your instruction.

Source: Copyright © 2014 by Piedmont Elementary School, Duluth, Minnesota. Used with permission.

Peer Coaching Pre- and Post-Observation Conference Worksheet

Peer Coaching	
Teacher: _____ **Peer Coach:** _____	
Observation Date and Time: _____	
Grade or Subject: _____	
Post-Observation Coaching Conversation Date and Time: _____	
Pre-Observation Planning Conference	
1. Student Outcomes • What do you want your students to know or do by the end of the lesson? • What essential questions are the students considering?	2. Assessment • How will you gather evidence of student learning?
Notes for Student Outcomes:	Notes for Assessment:
3. Instruction • What strategies will you use to reach your student outcomes?	4. Data Collection • What kind of data would be helpful for the peer coach to collect?
Notes for Instruction:	Notes for Data Collection:
Post-Observation Conference	
1. What went well? 2. What do you want to strengthen? 3. What are your next steps and why?	

Source: Copyright © 2014 by Piedmont Elementary School, Duluth, Minnesota. Used with permission.

Building a School of Collective Efficacy Rating Scale

Read each statement and reflect on how you rate in developing a school of collective efficacy. Then, determine next steps for growth.

Providing Shared Leadership	Strongly Disagree	Somewhat Disagree	Somewhat Agree	Strongly Agree
I know each of my staff member's strengths, passions, and how they would like to be involved in leadership opportunities in the school.				
Next Steps:				
I give my teachers choice and voice in the leadership opportunities they are a part of.				
Next Steps:				

Creating Collective Learning Opportunities	Strongly Disagree	Somewhat Disagree	Somewhat Agree	Strongly Agree
I use research to help guide the learning opportunities that take place in my school.				
Next Steps:				
I provide vicarious learning opportunities for my staff to observe strategies and practices prior to having to implement the strategies in their own classrooms.				
Next Steps:				
I plan for mastery experiences with my staff that allow staff members to practice with one another.				
Next Steps:				
I use peer coaching opportunities for my staff to observe and learn from one another.				
Next Steps:				

Creating a Positive School Climate	Strongly Disagree	Somewhat Disagree	Somewhat Agree	Strongly Agree
I am intentional about providing social support to my staff when evident they have stress or anxiety.				
Next Steps:				
I plan community building activities for my staff to deepen their relationships.				
Next Steps:				

Part Two

What Matters Most?

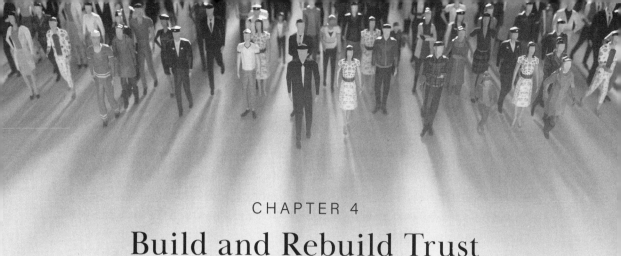

CHAPTER 4
Build and Rebuild Trust

*Trust is the glue of life. It's the most essential
ingredient in effective communication. It's
the foundational principle that holds all
relationships.*

—Stephen R. Covey

Katie Ann nervously anticipated stepping into a leadership role at an organization that was falling apart. She had read everything written about the organization in the newspaper and understood that Summit Special Education Center was in dire need of help. In fact, the headlines could not have been more discouraging.

"Summit Special Education Center: In Need of a Change"

"High Needs, High Turnover"

"Teachers Look for a Way Out"

But this was precisely what drew Katie Ann to the organization. She knew working at Summit Special Education Center could lend itself to stress and burnout. Special education teachers around the United States are known for higher rates of turnover than general education teachers (Samuels & Harwin, 2018). But this situation was different. From the outside looking in, Summit Special Education Center seemed to have it all: a brand-new state-of-the-art facility, reduced class sizes, and extended financial support. The school provided specially designed instruction and related services, with learning spaces, furniture, and security measures uniquely geared toward their students' needs. Summit Special Education Center was a place that students could call their own.

Katie Ann questioned how a school so wonderfully made for the unique needs of students could be so notorious for teacher dissatisfaction and turnover. It didn't take long for her to realize the teacher retention problem had nothing to do with the facility at all.

Within the first few days on the job, Katie Ann would learn most of her staff were forcibly placed at the school, leaving them disgruntled, resentful, and feeling like they had little control over their own destiny. Not knowing whom to trust, the staff resorted to meeting behind closed doors, gossiping about what was to come, and questioning the motives of the school administration. This only further created a culture of isolation and fear. Katie Ann quickly saw a pattern in the perpetual cycle of teacher turnover in her school. Teacher turnover caused forced placements. Forced placements caused unhealthy work conditions. Unhealthy work conditions caused more teacher turnover.

Katie Ann believed there was a better version of Summit Special Education Center just around the corner, and she had seen firsthand how organizations, communities, and individuals could change at breathtaking speed. She knew the school needed redemption, but most importantly, the school needed trust. So, minute by minute, hour by hour, Katie Ann worked to tear down the walls of distrust that her staff had worked so hard to build up. Katie Ann knew without trust, Summit Special Education Center would never live up to its full potential, and without trust, it would never break the vicious turnover cycle.

In this chapter, we discuss what trust is and why it matters before discovering several strategies on how to build and rebuild trust within your staff. You will then have the opportunity to assess how you build and rebuild trust and reflect on the impact of this on the wider school community.

What Is Trust?

As the leader in your school, you are in the greatest position to set the conditions for a trusting environment (Tschannen-Moran & Gareis, 2015). Trust influences one's ability to communicate, collaborate, and get things done. But what will it take for your staff to trust you, and what intentional actions are necessary to build trust among your staff? In this chapter, we place our attention on the question What matters most?—the fourth ripple of our Lasting Legacy model—by taking a closer look at the concept of trust (see figure 4.1).

Building and rebuilding trust should be intentionally embedded throughout your entire leadership journey. If teachers don't trust you, they will never fully believe in your teacher self-efficacy and collective efficacy efforts or genuinely consider you an authentic leader.

Figure 4.1: The fourth ripple in the Lasting Legacy model.

A quick review of trust in empirical literature underscores the elusiveness of this construct and points to a few commonalities of definition. Victoria Handford and Kenneth Leithwood (2013) explain that trust is built on things like "competence, consistency and reliability, openness, respect, and integrity" (p. 194). Other researchers assert trust is built on "some semblance of benevolence, care, competence, honesty, openness, reliability, respect, hope, and wisdom" (Kutsyuruba & Walker, 2015, p. 33). Perhaps the most compelling and frequently used definition of trust in schools comes from Megan Tschannen-Moran's (2014) book *Trust Matters: Leadership for Successful Schools*, where she defines trust as "one's willingness to be vulnerable to another based on the confidence that the other is benevolent, honest, open, reliable, and competent" (pp. 19–20). Tschannen-Moran (2014) goes on to explain, "Trust matters most in situations of interdependence, in which the interest of one party cannot be achieved without reliance on another" (p. 20). Sometimes your teachers need you to help them accomplish what they set out to do. If they're going to trust you, they're going to need to be able to answer the following questions.

- "Can I fully trust my leader to help me accomplish my goals?"
- "Can I rely on them in my time of need?"
- "Does my leader have the necessary skills to help me?"

Why Does Trust Matter?

Trust is a vital factor related to the success of your teachers' work lives, yet it is often forgotten in the teacher-turnover conversation. Several teacher turnover factors have a much more visible scope, meaning they are more easily seen or measured than the factor of trust. For instance, teacher working conditions are a prominent contributor to whether or not teachers will stay in their schools (Burkhauser, 2017; Johnson, Kraft, & Papay, 2012). But, as you unpack the components that comprise teacher working conditions, it's not hard to see that at the very core is the presence or absence of relational trust within the staff of the school building. In general, teacher working conditions consist of "the physical features of the workplace, the organizational structure, and the sociological, political, psychological, and educational features of the work environment" (Ladd, 2011, p. 237). Teacher retention scholar Helen F. Ladd (2011) explains that one of the premier working conditions related to teacher turnover is the collegial atmosphere in the school. Collegiality includes school leadership working *with* and *through* their staff, helping teachers believe in themselves, and relying on one another through collaborative efforts (Ladd, 2011).

The absence of trust undermines collegiality in schools. When teachers don't trust you as their leader, they are less likely to support any of your efforts, even when those efforts are valid and worthy of consideration. When teachers don't trust colleagues, they are less likely to collaborate and rely on one another in times of need. When teachers feel a lack of growth or collaboration, they are more likely to leave their job in search of another. Essentially, low trust produces low collegiality, a component that influences poor working conditions. Poor working conditions enable teacher turnover, and teacher turnover hinders the ability for teachers to build and sustain trusting relationships, thus creating a cycle of turnover as illustrated in figure 4.2.

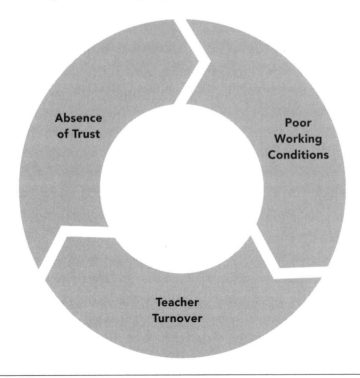

Figure 4.2: The cycle of teacher turnover.

Susan Moore Johnson, Matthew A. Kraft, and John P. Papay (2012) explain the problem leaders run into when their school becomes a high turnover school caused by the conditions in which they work, saying:

> Teachers are three times more likely to plan to transfer from schools with particularly poor conditions of work than are teachers whose work environment is of average quality. These high turnover rates erode efforts to foster meaningful collegial relationships, develop instructional capacity, and establish a strong organizational culture. (p. 31)

THREE-MINUTE PAUSE

What are the amens, ahas, or ideas swirling in your brain about building and rebuilding trust so far in this chapter?

How Do I Build and Rebuild Trust?

Chances are, whether you realize it or not, trust has played a significant factor in your leadership. Like Katie Ann in our opening story, you may be working with staff for whom suspicion and fear are ingrained in the culture, and you're losing teachers because of it. Or you may be looking for proven ways to continue building trust with an already strong staff. Perhaps you've lost trust with your staff and need to find a way to rebuild it. Whatever the reason, you need realistic and timely trust-building and rebuilding practices you can implement in your school. Leaders build and rebuild trust in their schools when they embody trust-building behaviors, build a narrative of trust among staff, prepare for difficult conversations, and rebuild trust through problem solving.

We use the remainder of this chapter to show you how to build and rebuild trust by walking you through specific actions Katie Ann took with her staff—actions that you can apply in your own setting.

INSIGHTS FROM THE FIELD

"When people are able to trust you, they see you as credible and feel that they can rely on you. If teams can trust each other, they tend to be much more productive and able to accomplish more of the tasks at hand. It can take time to build trust among a team, but trust can be lost rather quickly, resulting in an unmotivated team lacking morale. A strong leader not only proves their own trustworthiness but is able to trust others in order to be successful."

—School board member,
personal communication, July 27, 2020

Embody Trust-Building Behaviors

Katie Ann's step into leadership at Summit Special Education Center found her in an interesting predicament: seeking to build trust as the new leader of a staff while at the same time rebuilding trust between the members of the staff. Many of you have faced such a scenario and have found building and rebuilding trust are not always easy to do. Building trust involves taking risks. As the leader in your building, it is your responsibility to set the tone by putting yourself out there and taking the first risk (Keyes, 2019). Your staff's trust in you is directly related to how they perceive you, meaning you need to make sure your teachers can *see*, *hear*, and *feel* your trustworthiness. In his book *The Principal: Three Keys to Maximizing Impact*, Michael Fullan (2014) explains how to earn trust with your staff by saying:

> You can't talk your way into trust. I mean that you can only "behave" your
> way into it by naming, modeling, and monitoring your trustworthiness.
> You name trust as a value and norm that you will embrace and develop
> in the organization; you model it in your day-to-day actions; and you
> monitor it in your own and others' behavior. (p. 130)

You cannot just tell your staff to trust you. Building trust with your staff means you actually walk the talk, embodying trust-building behaviors and living them out in a consistent manner over time. Think back to Megan Tschannen-Moran's (2014) definition of trust that we provided earlier in this chapter in which she offers five trust-building facets that you can use to help name, model, and monitor your trustworthiness as a school leader. As you read through each facet, ask yourself, "Do I exhibit the traits of this facet? If so, how? If not, what am I missing?" Then, use the

"Facets of Trust Worksheet" at the end of the chapter (page 100) to further examine if you are a leader teachers can trust.

1. **Benevolence:** Leaders earn trust with their teachers when they show that they care for them (Tschannen-Moran, 2014). Such kindness can be exhibited through informal thank-you notes, phone calls on birthdays, and spoken acknowledgments.

2. **Honesty:** Leaders need to respectfully speak the truth. One off-the-cuff remark, one unspoken truth, or one little white lie can completely tarnish the trust between a principal and their staff. Honest principals consistently follow through with what they say they are going to do. Much of this has to do with your authenticity, the topic of our first chapter (Tschannen-Moran, 2014).

3. **Openness:** Leaders display openness to their staff when they share leadership and are willing to provide information when it's appropriate to do so. Openness is a reciprocal trait. When you open up to your staff, they will open up to you (Tschannen-Moran, 2014).

4. **Reliability:** Building trust requires consistency over time (Tschannen-Moran, 2014). Teachers need to rely on you time and time again. You are most reliable to your staff when your words and actions remain aligned even during the most difficult of circumstances.

5. **Competence:** "Competence is the ability to perform a task as expected, according to appropriate standards" (Tschannen-Moran, 2014, p. 35). Teachers need to know their principals can perform their job responsibilities as *they perceive them to be.* Your competence will be defined in various ways when you step up in situations when your staff members rely on you the most. This means your competence may look different to different people. For example, some of your teachers will base your competence off of your ability to handle student discipline, while others will base your competence off of your strength in instructional leadership. An awareness of you and your staff's perceptions of competence will be critical and can be accomplished through such things as listening sessions, a review with your staff about your own perceptions of your role, and checking in with your staff on a periodic basis.

The five trust-building facets are influenced by the nonverbal cues you are sending to your staff. How does your staff perceive the genuineness of your trust-building behaviors through your nonverbal communication? For Katie Ann, answering this question meant being cognizant in her approach to new situations from the very beginning to the very end of the school year. She routinely asked herself the following questions.

- "Am I using my facial expressions to show my teachers I am in support of them?"

- "Am I making eye contact with my teachers?"

- "Does my posture help demonstrate I am listening?"

- "Am I positioning my body using an open stance to show I am open to what they have to say?"

Build a Narrative of Trust Among Staff

While having self-awareness of the trust-building behaviors you embody is a vital first step to building trust with your staff, it's not enough for lasting trust within your building. You need to establish the conditions necessary to build a *culture* of trust. You do this by creating deliberate practices designed for staff to talk about and build on their strengths of trust already present. For example, Katie Ann knew that to stop the perpetual cycle of teacher turnover in her building, she needed to refocus her staff's narrative about the school. She wanted to help her staff have conversations about the positive things happening around them and use the conversations to plan for the future. She implemented an appreciative inquiry process. Megan Tschannen-Moran (2014) advocates for the use of *appreciative inquiry* when developing trust with staff, which she describes as "a process for fostering whole-system change by focusing on strengths and what is going well rather than on problems, gaps, or discrepancies between the aspirations of people and the current reality of their relationships" (p. 243). Appreciative inquiry thought leaders Jacqueline M. Stavros, Lindsey N. Godwin, and David L. Cooperrider (2016) suggest five questions leaders can ask their staff to promote positive organizational change on any topic in their school.

1. **Define:** "What generative topic do we want to focus on together?" (p. 105)

2. **Discover:** "When we have been at our best, what were we doing?" (p. 105)

3. **Dream:** "When we achieve our ideal state of success, what will it look like?" (p. 106)

4. **Design:** "How might we make our vision a reality?" (p. 107)

5. **Destiny:** "How do we continue to leverage our strengths to deliver on the promise dreams and ensure our system flourishes in the future?" (p. 107)

Katie Ann used Stavros, Godwin, and Cooperrider's (2016) five questions of appreciative inquiry during the first two staff meetings of the school year to focus on the topic of trust. For the Define phase of their first meeting, Katie Ann created and used the essential question "How do we develop long-lasting relationships among our staff?" to bring focus to the topic they would be working on together. During the Discover and Dream phases, she had her staff answer the corresponding questions found in the "Trust-Building Exercise" reproducible (page 101).

Katie Ann then divided her staff into groups of four and invited each person to share their individual answers and stories with their group. Katie Ann's leadership team collected the responses and compiled the work into several consistent themes.

As Katie Ann's staff reconvened at the second staff meeting, they reviewed the themes and focused on the Design and Destiny phases. In small groups, the staff brainstormed actionable steps they could take to realize their dream and indicators of success to measure their progress over time. Ultimately, Katie Ann's goal with this process was to reduce negative thinking in the area of trust and have her staff talk about one another in more positive ways.

INSIGHTS FROM THE FIELD

"As a leader, trust in a colleague should open the door to being approachable and allow the colleague to take risks in trying new things without the feeling of being judged or unnecessarily reprimanded. Trust should involve building a positive relationship with a colleague so that support and collaboration can be an important part of everyday interaction. Trust honors different approaches and creates a welcoming environment so that when correction is needed, it is respected, and when support is needed, it is honored and appreciated."

—Instructional coach,
personal communication, July 23, 2020

Prepare for Difficult Conversations

Most school leaders could tell you that building and maintaining trust are easy during times of harmony in a school. Those same leaders could also name specific times when a difficult conversation completely obliterated trust among staff. The reality is that trust is something quite easy to maintain—until it's not. In fact, a person can spend years building trust with colleagues only to lose that trust during one disagreement. For trust to remain constant in your school, you and your staff need to remain open, honest, and vulnerable even through the most contentious of times. For instance, when was the last time your staff were divided over an important school decision? How did they respond to the tension and conflict that often accompany varying opinions and perspectives? Did they continue to remain vulnerable, relying on one another even when they disagreed? Preparing your staff to thoughtfully navigate difficult conversations while still feeling like they are a part of a safe environment is essential to building and maintaining trust. To do this, you need to plan for your staff to *experience* moments of trusting each other before difficult conversations occur.

Biren A. Nagda (2019) offers a four-stage process called *intergroup dialogue* that can help you build trust among your staff through scaffolding by getting to know one another's unique experiences and perspectives before engaging in more difficult conversations. Each step of the process elevates the amount of vulnerability required of your staff. We encourage you to work through each stage of the process, remaining on one stage until your staff have fully embraced that stage and show readiness for the next stage (Nagda, 2019). After completing all stages, you may want to use the process for more short-term solutions.

Stage 1: Forming and Building Relationships

Building relationships requires providing the necessary conditions for your staff to get to know one another as people. Approach this stage with non-threatening discussion prompts and team-building activities. Establish agreed-on norms as a group and introduce your staff to the concept of *productive dialogue* to build trust (Nagda, 2019). We use the term productive dialogue to refer to having healthy conversations, being willing to listen to multiple perspectives, and seeking the understanding of others' viewpoints. Productive dialogue moves from surface-level connections to deeper conversations. Participants in productive dialogue realize that while they may not always agree with everything they hear, they may walk away with a deeper appreciation for someone else's perspective. Before moving on to the next stage, you want your staff to feel relaxed enough to listen to their colleagues and comfortable enough to share about themselves.

Stage 2: Exploring Differences and Commonalities of Experience

Explore unique similarities and differences of staff members, encouraging your staff to seek the perspectives of their colleagues, practice listening, and show empathy (Gurin, Nagda, & Zúñiga, 2013). Start with non-threatening topics that are conducive to highlighting similarities and differences. You may ask, for example, "What part of the school day is your favorite?" or "What is your favorite class to teach?" Then, transition to topics that will stretch your staff's vulnerability, asking such things as "What's the biggest mistake you've made at our school?" or "What is one way you hope to grow both personally and professionally this year?" Patricia Gurin, Biren A. Nagda, and Ximena Zúñiga (2013) encourage you to use small groups or pairs during this stage to prevent any dominant staff members from taking the dialogue hostage. During this stage, you want your staff to recognize that no matter how different they may be from one another, they also have similarities. And, no matter how similar they are to each other, they also have differences. You want your staff to recognize and value each other's differences and similarities before moving on to the next stage.

Stage 3: Exploring and Dialoguing About Difficult Topics

Begin to explore how people respond to more contentious topics by incorporating strategies from the first two stages and applying them to dialogue concerning something more difficult while continuously keeping relationships at the forefront. You may have to be explicit about this with your staff by reviewing norms and guidelines for dialogue (Gurin et al., 2013). During this stage, you want your staff to practice engaging in a difficult conversation while keeping in mind the value of each other and the concept of appreciating varying perspectives.

Stage 4: Action Planning and Alliance Building

As a staff, determine the next steps that will address the topic discussed in stage 3. As you brainstorm possible next steps, determine those that you can agree on working toward together. Alliances within your staff will begin to build as those involved work toward their agreed-on next steps. Remind your staff to honor the perspectives of others as they contribute to action planning and that alliances will be built when staff begin to rely on one another, trusting each other to achieve their goals. Intergroup dialogue is often a process that takes time, patience, and energy, but there are also times when intergroup dialogue can be used for more immediate needs. Figure 4.3 (page 96) shows an example of when Katie Ann used the process of intergroup dialogue with her staff to discuss the scheduling of school assemblies.

Rebuild Trust Through Problem Solving

Let's face it, even when you have worked on your school's narrative and implemented a process for building trust among staff, there will still be times when you will lose trust with each other. You cannot, however, allow missteps to completely alter the trust-building path you have started to pave. When trust is compromised, authentically rebuild the trust that was lost, even when it's not your fault or shouldn't be your problem. Rebuilding trust cannot and should not be something you choose to do when you have extra time. It's not a choice; it's an obligation leaders should conduct in a timely manner.

Stage	Example
Stage 1: Forming and building relationships	Katie Ann asks her staff to answer the following question: When is the best time for us to have school assemblies? Why?
Stage 2: Exploring differences and commonalities of experience	Katie Ann has her staff discuss in groups the differences and commonalities among their responses to the question asked in stage 1.
Stage 3: Exploring and dialoguing about difficult topics	Katie Ann then asks teams to submit dates and times they would like to have their monthly school assemblies, taking into consideration the perspectives they shared in stage 2. Teams request to rotate the day and time of the assemblies each month knowing staff members had differing perspectives of when assemblies would work best in their schedule.
Stage 4: Action planning and alliance building	The staff create a schedule for the assemblies for the entire school year.

Source: Adapted from Gurin et al., 2013.

Figure 4.3: Intergroup dialogue example.

For leaders, perhaps the most difficult part of rebuilding trust is when others have acted in an untrustworthy way. Consider this example. As a building principal, district administration has approached you with concerns that one of your grade-level teams is grouping students based on their ability, a model the district would like to move away from. They have asked you to facilitate their transition from using an ability-grouping model to using another model for meeting individual student needs based on best practices in research. You've met with your grade-level team and explained the situation. The team promises they will make changes and move away from their ability-grouping model.

A few weeks later, you are conducting a routine walk-through and notice the team has not moved away from ability grouping. In fact, it is evident your team has no plans to change its model at all. So, how do you hold your team accountable for its actions while at the same time helping rebuild the trust you've lost in the members? Figure 4.4 walks you through how Katie Ann approached this scenario in her school by using the PEACE problem-solving process (R. Schoenert, personal communication, February 16, 2019). PEACE stands for *plan* a conference; *empathize*; *attack* the problem, not the person; *cooperate*; and re-*establish*. A blank template of this model for you to use to engage in challenging trust rebuilding conversations in your school is found at the end of the chapter (page 102). We encourage you to post this in your office as a visible reminder to provide ongoing encouragement and direction when moving through the PEACE process.

What do I do?	What do I say?	Example
P: Plan a conference. Sit down face to face with your teacher and validate their thoughts, feelings, and emotions.	Ask: • "Can we talk about the _____ (name the issue)?"	Katie Ann asks to meet with the team to talk about the ability-grouping model. "Can we talk about what is happening with ability grouping for mathematics?"
E: Empathize with the teacher. Go into the conference with the goal of truly listening to the other person.	If you broke the trust, say: • "I'd like to explain why I . . ." • "You are probably curious why I . . ." • "You may be puzzled as to why I . . ." If the other person broke the trust, say: • "Help me understand the reason you . . ." • "I am curious as to why you . . ." • "I am puzzled as to why you . . ."	Katie Ann asks the team to share the reasons it continued to implement the ability-grouping model. "I need to be honest. I'm puzzled as to why you continued ability grouping even after our initial conversation?"
A: Attack the problem, not the person. Eliminate the need for blaming, keeping the focus on what the conversation truly needs to be about.	Say: • "Let's look at how we can solve this together."	Katie Ann asks her team to work with her to find other models to meet the students' needs other than ability grouping. "Let's take a look at a few alternative options we could use other than ability grouping."
C: Cooperate by identifying areas of agreement and disagreement and taking ownership in your part. Build a bridge and identify possible solutions.	Say: • "This is how I contributed to the problem . . ." • "Where do we agree and disagree?"	Katie Ann guides the team in exploring its areas of agreement and disagreement, trying to find common ground. "I realize I did not provide enough rationale for moving away from ability grouping. Let me share some reasons I believe we should do this, and then perhaps we could determine where we agree and where we differ."
E: Re-establish the relationship and emphasize reconciliation and not winning.	Say: • "Thank you for working *with* me. We will find a way to make this work together."	Katie Ann and the team find common ground and agree to continue to meet to problem solve through the situation. "I really believe in your team and know that together we can do what's best for kids. Let's keep meeting to make sure things are going all right for you."

Figure 4.4: PEACE problem-solving process example.

Reflection

You will find the "Building and Rebuilding Trust Rating Scale" at the end of the chapter (page 103). The rating scale will help you assess your current state of building and rebuilding trust, identify areas of strength and needs for improvement, and provide focus to your professional learning progress.

What About the Support Staff?

- Focus on building relationships early in the school year. Simple yet thoughtful exchanges through words of encouragement go a long way in showing staff that you care.

- Define expectations clearly and then trust staff to do what is expected. Be honest when you see a need for improvement.

- Address staff behaviors by taking all viewpoints into consideration, modifying and accommodating to their needs when it's necessary or appropriate to do so.

Conclusion

Throughout this chapter, we encouraged you to begin asking the question "What matters most?" by placing your focus on the concept of trust. Trust must be a priority communicated within every interaction. It builds positive behaviors and respect when navigating a staff through challenging circumstances. Much like it was for Katie Ann, trust needs to be a priority in your school, not simply another thing to do, but *the* thing to do. Your trust efforts will lift up your teachers, keep them working at your school, and will eventually instill a long-lasting legacy within them. You can do this when you embody trust-building behaviors, build a narrative of trust among the staff, prepare your staff for difficult conversations, and help rebuild trust using a proactive problem-solving approach.

Talk It Over: Reflection Guide for Discussions

Growing as a learner and leader takes thoughtful reflection. Interacting with this book's text and listening to the experiences of others will make you more fully aware of who you are as a leader and the steps you can take to grow. Thoughtful conversations take time and energy, but investing in one another through these conversations will establish the support group you will need when the going gets tough.

1. **Introducing yourself to the topic:** Have you witnessed any trustworthy leaders in your life? How have you experienced their leadership? How do these leaders stand out differently from other leaders?

2. **Looking inward:** When is a time you lost trust in a colleague? How did this happen? Was trust rebuilt?

3. **Making connections:** Take a moment to interact with the following statement by highlighting, underlining, or writing in the margins. Jot down questions or connections you have with the statement to your life, community, and world. Then, share out your thoughts.

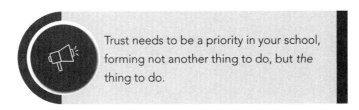

> Trust needs to be a priority in your school, forming not another thing to do, but *the* thing to do.

4. **Applying it in practice:** Growing as a leader takes steps of action. You can do that with confidence when you share openly with others, supporting one another in those steps. Reflect on the "Building and Rebuilding Trust Rating Scale" (page 103). Where is your greatest need for growth? What step will you take to grow in that area?

Facets of Trust Worksheet

Facets	Think-Aloud Questions	Key Trust Competencies	Reflection
Benevolence	Do I exhibit kindness and caring toward my teachers?	• I look out for my teachers' interests, and they look out for mine. • I care about my teachers. • I would not take actions that would harm my teachers.	*Example: I listen to my teachers and care about what is going on in their life. I give my teachers a voice and help them feel heard.*
Honesty	Is there a discrepancy between what I say and what I do?	• I do not say one thing and do another.	
Openness	Am I open with my communication to staff when appropriate?	• I sense that everything is out on the table, and I work hard to make sure the school does not have a secretive culture.	
Reliability	Do I do what I say I am going to do and follow through on promises and commitments to my teachers?	• I follow through, so my colleagues don't have to think about a plan B.	
Competence	Do I have the skills needed to do the task that is required?	• I am able to perform my job successfully and efficiently. • My teachers know they can come to me to help them get things done.	

Source: Adapted from Tschannen-Moran, M. (2014). Trust matters: Leadership for successful schools *(2nd ed.). San Francisco: Jossey-Bass.*

Trust-Building Exercise

Define: How Do We Develop Long-Lasting Relationships Among Our Staff?

Purpose: To identify the amazing things happening in our school by building on and recognizing strengths, envisioning future hopes, creating steps to achievement, and monitoring progress.

Staff Meeting 1 Directions: Please respond to the following questions by writing a list of no more than ten words or phrases for each category. The leadership team will be collecting your responses for future work.

- **Discover:** When we have been at our best developing long-lasting relationships among our staff, what were we doing?

  _____

  _____

  _____

  _____

- **Dream:** What would long-lasting relationships look like among our staff? What is your hope for our school when you think of developing long-lasting relationships?

  _____

  _____

  _____

  _____

Staff Meeting 2 Directions: After looking at the compiled themes, please respond to the following questions by writing a list of no more than ten words or phrases for each category.

- **Design:** What do you believe are the best ways for our school to build trust with one another? How can we make this a reality?

  _____

  _____

  _____

  _____

- **Destiny:** How can we use our staff's strengths to fulfill our dreams of developing long-lasting relationships among our staff? How will we know we are reaching our goals?

  _____

  _____

  _____

  _____

Source: Adapted from Stavros, J. M., Godwin, L. N., & Cooperrider, D. L. (2016). Appreciative inquiry: Organization development and the strengths revolution. In W. J. Rothwell, J. M. Stavros, & R. L. Sullivan (Eds.), Practicing organization development: Leading transformation and change *(4th ed., pp. 96–116). Hoboken, NJ: Wiley.*

PEACE Problem-Solving Template

PEACE Problem-Solving Example		
What do I do?	**What do I say?**	**My Plan**
P: Plan a conference. Sit down face to face with your teacher and validate their thoughts, feelings, and emotions.	Ask: • "Can we talk about the _____ (name the issue)?"	
E: Empathize with the teacher. Go into the conference with the goal of truly listening to the other person.	If you broke the trust, say: • "I'd like to explain why I . . ." • "You are probably curious why I . . ." • "You may be puzzled as to why I . . ." If the other person broke the trust, say: • "Help me understand the reason you . . ." • "I am curious as to why you . . ." • "I am puzzled as to why you . . ."	
A: Attack the problem, not the person. Eliminate the need for blaming, keeping the focus on what the conversation truly needs to be about.	Say: • "Let's look at how we can solve this together."	
C: Cooperate by identifying areas of agreement and disagreement and taking ownership in your part. Build a bridge and identify possible solutions.	Say: • "This is how I contributed to the problem . . ." • "Where do we agree and disagree?"	
E: Re-establish the relationship and emphasize reconciliation and not winning.	Say: • "Thank you for working *with* me. We will find a way to make this work together."	

Building and Rebuilding Trust Rating Scale

Read each statement and reflect on how you rate in building and rebuilding trust. Then, determine next steps for growth.

Embodying Trust-Building Behaviors	Strongly Disagree	Somewhat Disagree	Somewhat Agree	Strongly Agree
I am aware of the facets of trust and have assessed whether or not I embody each of these facets.				
Next Steps:				
I pay attention to my nonverbal communication.				
Next Steps:				

Building a Narrative of Trust Among Staff	Strongly Disagree	Somewhat Disagree	Somewhat Agree	Strongly Agree
I provide opportunities for my staff to reflect on and talk about their strengths and use those strengths to plan for the future.				
Next Steps:				

page 1 of 2

Preparing for Difficult Conversations	Strongly Disagree	Somewhat Disagree	Somewhat Agree	Strongly Agree
I promote healthy dialogue with my staff about difficult topics by creating a safe environment built on relationships.				
Next Steps:				

Rebuilding Trust Through Problem Solving	Strongly Disagree	Somewhat Disagree	Somewhat Agree	Strongly Agree
I am prepared to address the times when I have lost trust with my staff or my staff have lost trust with me.				
Next Steps:				

CHAPTER 5

Listen to Your People

*When we learn how to listen more deeply to
others, we can listen more deeply to ourselves.*

—*Parker J. Palmer*

There are times as leaders when we encounter experiences that give us insight and guidance to better leadership. These experiences often provide a subtle nudge in the right direction, reminding us of what matters most and how we can best lead those we are called to serve. For Michael, his experience of new insight and guidance came on a day he had much anticipated, but the experience ended up hitting him not like a gentle nudge but like a slap in the face. It was the day he got the results from his teachers' job satisfaction survey.

As principal of Westview High School, Michael was accustomed to receiving feedback from all kinds of stakeholders. Still, thinking about reading the responses to the job satisfaction survey made him feel nervous. He cared about his staff and the relationship he had with them. He wanted them to be effective teachers and to be happy working in his school. He knew he was in good standing with his staff, or at least he thought he was, so he remained hopefully optimistic about what was to come. Then he began to read the answers to the first open-ended question of the survey, "Do you feel heard by your administrator?"

> *"I wish I felt more heard. It's just Michael has so much going on. It's really hard to have a conversation with him. It seems like when I do, he is completely distracted by other things like his phone, emails, or the latest school crisis. It's like his mind is always thinking about something else, rarely in tune with what I am saying. I'm sure he's not trying to do this, but he's placing priority on his distractions over me. It makes me feel a little underappreciated."*

> *"Quite honestly, not so much. Every time I ask Michael to talk about a problem I have, he just wants to jump in with advice on what he would do in my situation. It would be helpful if he would just take the time to listen to me and place value in what I have to say."*

As Michael read comment after comment, it was evident there were times in his leadership that he was distracted, and this was having an impact on whether his teachers felt heard. It was also evident his knack for helping solve problems was not always appreciated like he thought it would be. But it wasn't until he read the last comment that Michael truly realized he had a listening problem.

> *"Do I feel heard by my administrator? Ha! Absolutely not! It seems like Michael only listens to what he wants to hear. How could a principal be so oblivious to the problems and concerns surrounding him? I can honestly say in my years of teaching under Michael's leadership, there have only been a few times when he actually took stock of what I had to say. He is usually so busy trying to fix us, trying to turn us into becoming who he wants us to be, that he completely neglects the roots of the problems we face. Michael's out of touch, and people are sick of it. It's no wonder teachers are dropping like flies around here. Who knows, maybe I'll be next."*

Michael was stunned by these comments. With responses like this, there was no denying he had a serious problem listening meaningfully to his teachers. It was obvious to him that he needed to address the differences between the way he listened and the type of listening his teachers *needed* from him.

Your situation is no different. Your teachers *need* to be heard. Without question, listening to your teachers takes time, effort, and energy that, quite honestly, you may not always have. But, if you want your teachers to feel heard, understood, and valued, you need to turn off your distractions, stop trying to fix your teachers, and take a minute to step into their shoes. As renowned leadership author Stephen R. Covey (2004) puts it:

> All the well-meaning advice in the world won't amount to a hill of beans if we're not addressing the real problem. And we'll never get to the problem if we're so caught up in our own autobiography, our own paradigms, that we don't take off our glasses long enough to see the world from another point of view. (p. 250)

Teachers feel valued when we give them a voice, and we give them a voice when we *actually* listen to them, attempting to hear them from *their* perspectives and understand their circumstances through *their* lenses. That's why it's time for you to capitalize on one of the most powerful tools in your leadership arsenal: listening. Because if you don't listen to your teachers, they'll go find a leader who will.

In this chapter, we discuss what empathic listening is and why it matters before discovering several strategies to develop your listening skills as a leader. You will then have the opportunity to assess your level of empathic listening and reflect on the impact of your abilities on the wider school community.

What Is Empathic Listening?

We all have a life story to tell. Our life stories are molded by our personal experiences shaping who we are and defining our values, beliefs, assumptions, and philosophies. Our life stories are unique to us, rarely fully understood by those around us. Yet, when we open up and share our experiences with others, we enrich their lives by offering new or different ways of thinking and being. This is no different for your teachers. Each of them has a life story filled with ups and downs, joys and sorrows. These stories influence how they perceive the world and how they respond in situations in the course of their work as teachers. If we as leaders want to truly understand *who our teachers are* and *what they need*, we have to start listening to them in a way that enables us to empathize with where they are coming from. In this chapter, we continue to focus on the question "What matters most?" by placing our attention on *how* we should listen to our teachers (figure 5.1).

Figure 5.1: The fourth ripple in the Lasting Legacy model.

Researchers use a wide variety of terms to describe the type of listening we're referring to, such as listening with compassion, listening with empathy, and empathic listening. In his book *The 7 Habits of Highly Effective People*, Stephen R. Covey's (2004) well-known Habit 5—"Seek first to understand, then to be understood" (p. 235)—is grounded in the concept of empathic listening, which he suggests is "the highest form of listening" (p. 240).

Empathy, a significant part of empathic listening, is the process of stepping into another's world, seeking to understand what this other person is thinking, feeling, and understanding as their own truth. Empathic listening takes empathy one step further by incorporating the communicative process of listening to *show* another individual an understanding of their perspective. Empathic listening can be defined as "a way of being with a person so that the person believes and feels respected without judgment" (Perera-Diltz, 2017, p. 966). There is no doubt some of your teachers have made mistakes to the point by which they could be judged. Some have possibly said hurtful things to you or about you, some have blatantly disregarded your advice, and some have even compromised your ability to trust them. But, listening to your staff with empathy requires you to be open to your teachers anyway, setting aside your preconceived judgments and forgiving them regardless of their previous behavior (Boske, Osanloo, & Newcomb, 2017).

Why Does Empathic Listening Matter?

Leaders who listen to their teachers will improve their own personal growth and understanding of others while showing others they truly care about who they are and what they have to say. Listening will help you understand your teachers' inner workings and what drives them to succeed. This is important considering teacher job satisfaction is directly tied to internal motivation, meaning the things *within* your teachers that drive their desire to achieve goals are similar to those things that give your teachers fulfillment in their jobs.

According to self-determination theory, the internal motivation of your staff derives from three fundamental components: (1) competence, (2) autonomy, and (3) relatedness (Deci, Olafsen, & Ryan, 2017). Your staff will be internally motivated when they set personal goals and work toward achieving them (competence), feel a sense of ownership and belonging with other people within the school (relatedness), and are given the freedom to use their professional discretion when they see fit (autonomy). Yet all too often, teachers feel like they have little control or say over the things that matter most to them, such as curriculum, instruction, and assessment decisions, how to best teach certain topics, and the materials they use within their classrooms. Such a lack of autonomy can result in job dissatisfaction and ultimately drive teachers out of the profession (Sutcher et al., 2016).

The problem often lies with administrators failing to listen to their teachers in a way that helps their teachers *feel* like their voices matter. For example, a survey from Educators for Excellence (2020) asked 1,500 teachers if they felt school administrators heard them. Only 32 percent of teachers surveyed believed that within their school "their perspective [was] represented a 'great deal' in policy decisions" (Educators for Excellence, 2020, p. 31). This is a concern considering "teachers who perceived that they had more influence over their school's policies were more likely to remain in the profession, and in their schools" (Podolsky, Kini, Bishop, & Darling-Hammond, 2016, p. 40).

Teachers are educated and trained to have expertise in their professional practice, and they want to be treated as though they do. Yet, while high standards and teacher accountability are on the rise, honoring teacher professionalism and autonomy is declining (Ingersoll, May, & Collins, 2019). In a 2015 interview between Owen Phillips (2015) and leading teacher retention researcher Richard Ingersoll, Ingersoll explains the importance of teacher voice and its implications in teacher retention by saying:

> One of the main factors [of teacher retention] is the issue of voice, and having say, and being able to have input into the key decisions in the building that affect a teacher's job. This is something that is a hallmark of professions. It's something that teachers usually have very little of, but it does vary across schools and it's very highly correlated with the decision whether to stay or leave.

What makes all of this difficult is the fact that the autonomous needs of staff vary from one school to another, and in many cases from one staff member to the next. But, without listening to your staff members, you may never know what it is they most desire and need that gives them the internal motivation to feel competent in their jobs, the freedom to have power over their own destinies, and the feeling of belonging within your school. The truth is, we will never be able to walk entirely in our teachers' shoes. We will never fully understand *their* experiences and what they are dealing with on a daily basis. But it is within our power to provide the conditions necessary to increase our teachers' internal motivation, and that starts with giving them space to be heard.

THREE-MINUTE PAUSE

What are the amens, ahas, or ideas swirling in your brain about listening to your people so far in this chapter?

_____

_____

_____

_____

_____

_____

_____

How Do I Listen as a Leader?

Are you listening to your teachers with empathy? Are you seeking to understand their perspectives outside of your own agenda? Can you limit your impulse toward fixing your teachers and instead try to understand where they are coming from? Can you set aside your distractions and provide a space for your teachers to be heard? Much like Michael from our opening story, if you are not being thoughtful about the way you are listening to your teachers, you may not know how they're feeling, and you may have to find out the hard way.

There are two steps Michael, from the story at the beginning of the chapter, could take to help his teachers feel heard. These are steps you'll be able to incorporate with your staff: (1) developing listening skills and (2) conducting listening sessions.

Develop Listening Skills

Let's say one of Michael's teachers approaches him about a problem she is having with a colleague. How could he listen to his teacher in a way that makes the teacher feel heard? A typical school leader's response would be to help that teacher find solutions to the problem. This is because most school leaders have a natural inclination toward helping people. However, it's not always necessary or appropriate to do this. Before jumping in to fix the problem, take a step back and listen to what the teacher has to say. By listening intently, you may guide the staff member into discovering their own answers to the concern brought forth (D. Sabol, personal communication, July 19, 2019).

Researchers emphasize three stages to be cognizant of when listening (Bodie, 2011). *Sensing*, the first stage of listening, includes listening to what the speaker is saying and interpreting the speaker's feelings or emotions based on their nonverbal cues (Bodie, 2011). Sensing helps the listener realize where the speaker is coming from. Considering the many tasks you are responsible for as an administrator, this could be difficult, and it could be easy to start thinking about other items on your to-do list. However, it's important to block out the distractions and stay attentive to what someone is saying to you. Also, try not to prep yourself for what you are going to say while the speaker is speaking as you may miss key information that they are sharing (McRae & Nainby, 2015).

Processing information, the next stage of listening, requires seeing, hearing, taking note of important verbal and nonverbal details from the speaker, and linking previous knowledge (Bodie, 2011). As an empathic listener, it's important for you to set your opinions aside while listening and remain in the moment. When you start to pass judgments on the person based on what you're hearing, you will quickly fall away from understanding the speaker's point of view (Kimble & Bamford-Wade, 2013). As you process what you've heard, we recommend asking yourself, "How would I feel if I were in their situation?" Ultimately, understanding what is being said from the speaker's perspective, not your own, is most valuable (Perera-Diltz, 2017).

Responding to the speaker, the third stage of listening, may include follow-up questions, clarifications, or echoing what the speaker has said in your own words to establish clarification (Bodie, 2011; Storring, 2016). At this point, you want your speaker to know you are stepping into their shoes and you are empathizing with what they have to say. We caution you here to understand that your words alone do not carry enough weight for your speaker to fully believe you are listening to them. Be mindful of the nonverbal messages you are sending, such as the way you position your body, your eye contact, and the type of facial expressions you make. These nonverbal messages often communicate more than words.

So, what do these stages look like in action? Let's walk through how Michael would approach each of these stages, using the example of a teacher coming to him about a problem with a colleague.

Sensing

As the teacher approaches Michael, she begins to explain how her colleague wasn't open to her thoughts and ideas. Michael closes his computer screen, positions his body in an open posture, and initiates eye contact. While he listens, Michael is attentive to his teacher's verbal and nonverbal messages, such as tone of voice, the words she is speaking, and her facial expressions. He asks himself questions such as, "What am I hearing and seeing?" "How is my teacher feeling?" and "What does this tell me about the message being communicated?"

Processing

To stay fully engaged, Michael waits to formulate how he will respond until his teacher is finished speaking. While his initial reaction is to judge the situation based on previous interactions between the two teachers, he waits, allowing his teacher to fully explain her perspective. Michael then processes the information, trying to understand the perspective of his teacher by asking himself, "How would I feel if my coworker didn't place value in what I had to say?"

Responding

Michael wants his teacher to feel heard. However, he needs to be cautious not to make assumptions, so he probes for a deeper understanding using simple statements and questions such as, "I hear frustration in your voice. Could you tell me a little bit more about what happened?" He also repeats and clarifies what he is hearing by saying, "I heard you say the two of you disagreed about how to use the remaining budget for your department. Tell me about that." After Michael responds, he then listens to his teacher, starting the three stages all over again.

There will be unique circumstances when you cannot or should not listen to a teacher. If your teacher is unable to maintain some semblance of a professional dialogue, you may need to end the conversation and plan to resume it at another time. Also, you're not always going to agree with what your teachers are saying when you are listening to them. But, even if you disagree with them, you can still honor their perspectives by helping them feel heard. The key is following the stages of listening and remaining open and honest with your teachers after you have heard them out.

INSIGHTS FROM THE FIELD

"One must listen with their ears, eyes, and heart. By directly looking at the teacher and not being distracted by other tasks, the connection is made between you, the listener, and the teacher, forming the collaboration and respect needed in any relationship. Teachers don't always know what they are asking for or have an answer for their problem or situation. It is important to remember that the teacher may not be looking for a solution but just for someone to listen, hear what they are saying, and ask if there is anything they need from you."

—Principal, personal communication, August 11, 2020

Conduct Listening Sessions With Staff

While developing listening skills is an important step in helping your teachers feel heard, you should also set aside time for teachers to share their perspectives in a more formal manner. One of the most powerful structured listening processes is listening sessions for staff. We refer to *listening sessions* as explicitly defined times devoted to listening and understanding the perspectives of your teachers on a specific topic. Let's say Michael needs to understand his teachers' perspectives on the implementation of new grading practices in the school. Knowing his teachers would want a say in the matter, he schedules a time for the staff to meet and share their perspectives with him. During the listening session, Michael would follow a process similar to the one detailed in the following sections.

Introduction

Welcome the teachers and acknowledge them for taking the time to be a part of the listening session. Reassure the group that there may be questions about the topic being addressed and that before the listening session begins, you will share all of the information you know about the topic up until this point. Let your teachers know that nobody has all of the answers, so it's important to keep an open mind when sharing.

Topic Introduction

Share the topic of the session with your teachers and let them know that while your role is to do the majority of the listening, you will be refocusing the group if they head in a different direction than the topic. To help with this, administrators can use a co-facilitator for the session or introduce the *parking lot* method, where teachers write down topics not related to the issue on Post-It notes and post them in a pre-determined space. These ideas are addressed either at a future session or individually with the teacher.

Presentation

Share the background information on the topic so that everyone has the same information. Also, share the norms and expectations of the listening session (for example, respect the process, respect yourself, and respect each other). For this step, it's helpful to have your teachers submit questions about the topic prior to the listening session. You can group their questions according to themes and address these during the presentation.

Listening Session

Open the floor for teachers to share their perspectives on the topic. Start with a question such as, "What experiences have you had with (the topic)?" After teachers have given their perspectives, ask, "What would you like to see happen with (the topic) and why?" For organizational purposes, it's helpful to have a procedure for participants to know who will speak next. You can have your staff sit in a circle, raise their hands, or use a talking stick to pass around. You can also provide an option for your teachers to write their thoughts down on an index card to be read aloud by a volunteer.

Next Steps

Share with the staff what will be done with the feedback you've gathered during the session.

Conclusion

Thank your teachers once again for attending the listening session and let them know that you value their voices and that their perspectives will help the school community learn and grow together.

Principals use listening sessions for a variety of reasons. Some choose to build them into their weekly or monthly routine, adding them to the school schedule and using them to provide teacher voice on timely issues. Other principals may prefer to use listening sessions during times of uncertainty, conflict, or when a problem needs to be solved. A discussion of tough topics within the listening session requires a wait time to help teachers process, so embrace the silence (Waks, 2015). You'll find there will be times you will actually need to speak during the listening session. We would encourage you to provide answers to questions using factual information such as student demographic data or budget numbers. When you're asked an open-ended question, refrain from sharing your opinions. Instead, remind your staff of the purpose of the listening session and then encourage them to share their perspectives once again.

INSIGHTS FROM THE FIELD

"The key for me is to be cognizant of when I am *not* listening to understand, and quickly move myself to that place. True listening involves looking at the person, giving them respectful acknowledgement of what they are saying, asking clarifying questions, and at times, summarizing their words to assure them they have been understood. This should be easy and natural—it is not. It takes practice, but the rewards in how listening refines and deepens our relationships are worth it. One of the key distinguishing factors, in my experience, of how people describe leaders they admire and those they don't involves listening. Listening to what we value, listening to our complaints, listening to what we think the solutions are, listening to our expertise, sometimes just listening to us vent—and not just listening in one ear and out the other, but listening to understand, and remembering and following up and asking to hear more."

—Coordinator,
personal communication, August 1, 2020

Reflection

At the end of the chapter (page 117), you will find the "Listening to Your People Rating Scale." The rating scale will help you assess your current state of listening to your teachers, identify areas of strength and needs for improvement, and provide focus to your professional learning progress.

What About the Support Staff?

- Offer opportunities for support staff to ask questions either in a one-to-one setting, during a group meeting, or by using an anonymous questionnaire tool. There will be times when your support staff will not be present to share their voice, so find creative ways to gather their thoughts and bring them to the table when they're not present.

- Professional growth is paramount to every position in the school. Ask your support staff what they feel would be most beneficial for them to succeed in their job. Help cover absences when professional development needs arise.

- Hold open conversations about students, procedures, and, to some degree, scheduling, seeking to understand their perspectives in order to make an informed decision.

Conclusion

Throughout this chapter, we encouraged you to continue answering the question "What matters most?" by looking at how you listen to your teachers. Your teachers want to be heard, have opportunities to share, and feel like their perspective is valued, meaning you have to give them a voice. But helping your teachers feel like they have a voice is about so much more than letting your teachers speak. Listening is about empathizing, seeking to understand another's perspective, and placing value in what you hear. When you authentically listen from your true self, your teachers will know you have their best interests at heart, and they will know you care. When they know you care, they will open themselves up to you, trust in you, and allow you to influence them through your leadership. Start to help your teachers feel heard by developing your own listening skills and creating platforms such as listening sessions to use those skills.

Talk It Over: Reflection Guide for Discussions

Growing as a learner and leader takes thoughtful reflection. Interacting with this book's text and listening to the experiences of others will make you more fully aware of who you are as a leader and the steps you can take to grow. Thoughtful conversations take time and energy, but investing in each other through these conversations will establish the support group you will need when the going gets tough.

1. **Introducing yourself to the topic:** Share a time when you felt like your perspective was truly heard by someone else. How did this feel? Why is this important?

2. **Looking inward:** Are you able to step into the shoes of your teachers, listening to them with empathy? What challenges do you face when trying to listen to your teachers?

3. **Making connections:** Take a moment to interact with the following statement by highlighting, underlining, or writing in the margins. Jot down questions or connections that you have with the statement to your life, community, and world. Then, share out your thoughts.

Without listening to your staff members, you may never know what it is they most desire and need that gives them the internal motivation to feel competent in their jobs, the freedom to have power over their own destiny, and the feeling of belonging within your school. The truth is, we will never be able to walk entirely in our teachers' shoes. We will never fully understand their experiences and what they are dealing with on a daily basis. But it is within our power to provide the conditions necessary to increase our teachers' internal motivation, and that starts with giving them space to be heard.

4. **Applying it in practice:** Growing as a leader takes steps of action. You can do that with confidence when you share openly with others, supporting one another in those steps. Reflect on the "Listening to Your People Rating Scale." Where is your greatest need for growth? What step will you take to grow in that area?

Listening to Your People Rating Scale

Read each statement and reflect on how you rate in listening to your teachers. Then, determine next steps for growth.

Developing Listening Skills	Strongly Disagree	Somewhat Disagree	Somewhat Agree	Strongly Agree
When I listen to my teachers, I am attentive to their verbal and nonverbal cues.				
Next Steps:				
When I listen to my teachers, I block out distractions around me.				
Next Steps:				
I seek the perspectives of my teachers and refrain from passing judgments while I listen.				
Next Steps:				
I respond to my teachers with empathy by being mindful of my own verbal and nonverbal cues.				
Next Steps:				

Conducting Listening Sessions With Staff	Strongly Disagree	Somewhat Disagree	Somewhat Agree	Strongly Agree
I seek the perspectives of my staff by scheduling defined times to listen to them.				
Next Steps:				

CHAPTER 6

Develop a Shared Vision

*It's important that we focus more on what we
need to be than on what we need to do.*

—Max De Pree

As Cara walked out of her building's leadership team meeting, she suddenly realized she had quite possibly reached the lowest point in her twenty-eight-year teaching career. But it wasn't caused by the fact that she was now the senior-most teacher in her building or that her school was moving on to a new principal for the fourth straight year. While both of these things were going to take some getting used to, they weren't the things weighing heavily on her mind. Rather, it was the comment she had heard during the meeting that played over and over in her head: "We now have the greatest achievement gap in the state." Cara knew working in a high-poverty school was not without its challenges. But honestly, could another teaching staff even come close to displaying the care and compassion toward its students that they had? Would any other staff give up their nights and weekends just to support their students a little bit more than they could during a normal school day?

While Cara wondered what more it would take to narrow the ever-increasing achievement gap, a thought occurred to her: Could her efforts, and those of her colleagues, actually be doing more harm than good? It seemed to her that their hard work only resulted in high rates of stress, burnout, and disappointment rather than in student achievement. In fact, Cara was so used to watching her colleagues work to the point of exhaustion that by the end of the year, she was rarely surprised to find many of them were in search of a job that didn't take such an emotional toll.

Cara considered what was missing in the staff's hard work at her school. She realized that it seemed like much of the staff wanted to make a difference, but single-handedly, rather than as a group. In fact, much of the hard work done throughout the building was done in isolation, each teacher moving in the direction they believed would best support their students. Because of this, the school rarely headed in a common direction and rarely unified under one common cause. From her experience, Cara knew individual efforts wouldn't be enough to close the largest achievement gap in the state, and individual efforts wouldn't reduce a high case of teacher burnout. Most importantly, individual efforts wouldn't provide the kind of support that their students needed. Cara was also quite certain that relying on the efforts of individuals was ingrained in the culture of her school and there was nothing anyone could do to turn her school around. That is, until the day her new boss pulled the staff together and proclaimed, "Here's what I know. The odds are stacked against us, and many people, ourselves included, think we face an insurmountable task. I am only one person. You are only one person. None of us can do this alone. The only way we succeed is to succeed together. We must unite as one!"

Cara watched with fascination as her new leader did what she had imagined impossible, and breathed new life into her down and nearly defeated colleagues by helping them find a shared vision that would unite all of them for years to come.

Much like Cara and her colleagues, the teachers in your building *want* to make a difference in the lives of students. In fact, many of them are going above and beyond their call of duty to do just that. But are they moving in the same direction *together*? Do they even know where their efforts should be taking them, and will they have a clue when they've arrived at their destination? There is no question your staff are working hard, but if they're not headed in the same direction together, their work may not be as impactful as it could be. This can influence your teacher retention efforts.

In this chapter, we discuss what vision is and why it matters before discovering several strategies on how to develop and maintain a shared vision. You will then have the opportunity to assess your school's current shared vision and reflect on the impact of this vision on the wider school community.

What Is Vision?

In this final chapter, we take one last look at the question, "What matters most?" by exploring how to create a shared vision in your school (see figure 6.1). Each of the previous chapters help set the stage for bringing your staff to this point: working together toward a shared vision. A compelling shared vision provides meaning and purpose to your staff and is a primary force for teacher retention. While defined in a variety of ways across leadership literature in some way, shape, or form, a vision will help answer the question, What do we want to become as a staff and as a school?

Figure 6.1: The fourth ripple in the Lasting Legacy model.

According to school leader and author Timothy D. Kanold (2011), a compelling school vision "describes how good we can become and paints a picture of what it will look like when we get there" (p. 12). James M. Kouzes and Barry Posner (2009) emphasize the need for the vision to be a collective vision that encompasses the unique perspective of each individual in the organization. They explain "constituents want visions of the future that reflect their own aspirations. They want to hear how their dreams will come true and their hopes will be fulfilled" (Kouzes & Posner, 2009, p. 21). Having a shared vision means we find a way as leaders to unite our staff toward one common destination while at the same time embracing the differences within the group.

A shared vision often starts as small as a seed, prompting something deep within you and your staff to recognize a need for change. As we plant that seed, we are thoughtful about where and when to plant, knowing optimal conditions will help the vision grow. We give the seed nourishment and time, allowing it to evolve and transform into something unifying, a collection of hopes, dreams, and aspirations of the entire school community. Eventually, that seed may grow into something much larger as it takes hold, multiplies, and flourishes. Along the way, we take care of weeding outside distractions. We prune policies and procedures no longer aligned with where our school is heading. As the leader of your school, *you* must be the caretaker of the vision. Without you, the shared vision will not grow or survive on its own.

When a shared vision is alive and well within your school, it will influence how your staff interact with one another, the things they choose to focus on, what they deem important and unimportant, and the kinds of decisions they'll make on a daily basis. Leaders who want to leave behind a lasting legacy are bound and determined to leave their school a little better than they found it by helping develop and maintain a vision that can stand the test of time.

Why Does a Shared Vision Matter?

Research points to the compounding effects a shared vision can have on teacher retention and, ultimately, the sustainment of success in your school. Teachers are more likely to commit to their work when they have a collective belief in the direction they are heading (Chai, Hwang, & Joo, 2017). As their commitment grows, so does their intent to stay in their teaching position (Mack, Johnson, Jones-Rincon, Tsatenawa, & Howard, 2019). In fact, a well-known teacher retention study (Allensworth, Ponisciak, & Mazzeo, 2009) makes clear the following with regard to teacher retention:

> Rates are 4 to 5 percentage points higher in schools where teachers report a strong sense of collective responsibility among teachers—where there is a shared commitment among the faculty to improve the school so that all students can learn—compared to schools serving similar students but without a sense of collective responsibility. (p. 25)

Ultimately, when teachers stay in their positions, they elevate the factors related to sustaining and achieving a vision such as trusting relationships, developing shared understandings, and building a cohesive community (Simon & Johnson, 2015). Research also shows vision positively influences teacher retention factors such as job satisfaction (Erdem, İlğan, & Uçar, 2014), stress (Haydon, Leko, & Stevens, 2018), and emotional well-being (Lambersky, 2016).

Research findings point to a lack of vision as a factor associated with teacher turnover (Carver-Thomas & Darling-Hammond, 2017). That's why providing a vision for your staff without gathering their input could be one of your most critical oversights as a school administrator. When we don't seek to understand the personal visions of our teachers, many of them won't feel like they have a stake in the game. We need to trust that our teachers have the capacity to dream about a better future for themselves and their students within our schools. Unfortunately, common practices of vision development all but neglect the voices of those that have the most impact in the classroom—the teachers. Roland S. Barth (as cited in Sergiovanni & Green, 2015) explains how teachers' personal visions are often lost when teachers are not explicitly involved in establishing the direction for the school. He states:

> All of us who entered teaching brought with us a conception of a desirable school. Each of us had a personal vision and was prepared to work, even fight, for it. Over time, our personal visions became blurred by the

visions, demands, and requirements of others. Many teachers' visions are now all but obliterated by external prescriptions. (Sergiovanni & Green, 2015, p. 228)

As you read Barth's quote, think about your role as a school administrator. Are you adding to or taking away from the personal visions of your teachers? When teachers don't feel like their personal vision is embedded into the overarching vision of the school, they will not embrace the vision and will never fully realize its meaning regardless of how great the vision may be. Kanold (2011) emphasizes this point by saying, "All stakeholders must own the vision, and if they don't have a voice in its development, they will never completely honor it" (p. 19). So, how do we find a way to honor our teachers' individual dreams for the future while uniting an entire staff to work toward a common destination?

Consider an orchestra. Each member of the orchestra has a role, using their individual talents to create a unique sound. Some set the technical aspects of rhythm and tempo. Others provide the melody or harmony. When played alone, each instrument has the capacity to make its own music. But, as part of an orchestra, each instrument has a greater purpose, and individual talent combines to create something an individual could not make on their own. Your teachers each have a picture of what they think a great school looks like. They also have talents that can help them realize their visions. Much like a successful orchestra, a shared vision requires a perfect combination of unity and individuality. Just as the orchestra members rely on the guidance of their conductor to lead them to one common destination—the successful presentation of a piece of music—you must do the same with your school.

INSIGHTS FROM THE FIELD

"The vision gives me the purpose and direction to take as I plan my course of action with the end in mind. A vision has to not only be well articulated and understood, it must also be shared by those who are charged with the task of taking you to that destination. There has to be buy-in and endorsement of the path to the destination by the stakeholders of the organization in order for it to be complete."

—Principal, personal communication, August 19, 2020

THREE-MINUTE PAUSE

What are the amens, ahas, or ideas swirling in your brain about creating a vision so far in this chapter?

_____

_____

_____

_____

_____

_____

_____

How Do I Develop and Maintain a Shared Vision?

What is prompting your staff to say that things could be different in your school? Is there a seed you are willing to plant, care for, and grow? Are you finding ways for your staff to unite toward one common destination while at the same time placing value in their differing perspectives? There is no doubt it will take time and effort to plant a shared vision with those you lead, but making a shared vision a reality will impact your school for years to come. If you plant the seed, you will reap the harvest, and you can do so by discovering the personal visions of individuals within your school, uniting the personal visions into one shared vision, and taking the shared vision well beyond the vision statement.

Discover the Personal Visions Within Your School

A shared vision for your school should begin with your understanding of your teachers' personal visions and their understanding of each other's personal visions. Start by asking a series of simple questions designed to recognize each staff member's unique lived experiences, needs, and hopes for the future. Then, provide time for your staff to reflect on their personal visions for the future by using a worksheet like the "Personal Vision Exercise" found at the end of the chapter (page 130). Give your staff large sheets of chart paper to prepare a visual of their personal vision based on their responses to the exercise.

Giving your staff time to consider their personal vision does two things. First, it sends a message to staff that they are invited to the process and that their perspectives matter. Second, it gives you an idea of where your staff are coming from, their personal priorities, and how you can help align those with the direction of the school.

Unite Personal Visions Into One Shared Vision

When individuals have completed their personal visions for the future, it's time for the staff to focus on the important work of creating a shared vision. After going over general norms and expectations, we recommend guiding your staff through a shared visioning process using the following essential questions.

What Visions Do We Share as a Small Group?

Seat staff members in small groups and remind the groups to honor all voices and be mindful of setting aside personal biases and assumptions while listening to their colleagues. In each group, have staff members take turns sharing their personal vision stories while the rest of the group listens. While listening, staff members should note any common words or phrases among the group. When each member of the group has shared their personal vision, ask, "What visions do we share as a small group?" The group should combine the commonalities of their visions together to create a shared vision poster. At this point, they do not have to write a vision statement. Instead, have them put down on paper what seem to be the most consistent ideas of the group. Any and all ideas are welcome and valued. If staff members have disagreements, encourage them to leave all options on the table.

What Visions Do We Share as a Whole Staff?

Have each group hang its shared vision poster on the wall for all to see. Then, ask the question, "What visions do we share as a whole staff?" To answer this, have the whole staff conduct a gallery walk, going from poster to poster observing similarities and differences between each group. Then, guide your staff through a conversation about what they noticed.

Where Do We Go From Here?

Conclude the shared vision session by asking, "Where do we go from here?" You want to continue honoring individual perspectives even when they differ. Have your staff complete a reflection sheet such as the one shown at the end of the chapter (page 131). Let them know your leadership team will use this information and the shared vision posters to craft a shared vision statement.

After the shared visioning session is complete, have your leadership team craft a shared vision statement. Chances are your leadership team may struggle to encapsulate *every* idea from the shared visioning session in one simple phrase or sentence, so remind team members to keep it simple, knowing this can be an iterative process. Vision consultant Jesse Lyn Stoner (n.d.) suggests your leadership team should solicit feedback from staff prior to making final determinations of the vision statement. Thoughtfully consider your staff's concerns, knowing you may have to go back to the drawing board if several common concerns arise.

Go Beyond the Crafting of a Shared Vision Statement

A shared vision may require your teachers to accept a vision contrary to their personal desires or traditional practices. That's why the only way a shared vision will work in your school is if it seems worth it to them, and it will only begin to seem worth it if you show your staff you are also committed to the cause. However, vision modeling doesn't have to just be from you. You'll want to stand back and spotlight prominent school heroes whose actions and behaviors align with what it will take for your staff to achieve their shared vision. Lee G. Bolman and Terrence E. Deal (2013) emphasize the importance cultural heroes play on influencing how we act in our schools by stating, "We carry lessons of teachers, parents, and others with us. Their exploits, animated through stories, serve as guides to choices we make in our personal lives and at work" (p. 253).

Whom in your school community does your staff hold in high esteem? Does this person live their life according to the shared vision you are trying to achieve? Vision heroes may be present or past teachers, secretaries, support staff, or students who stand out because of who they are and what they stand for. Your heroine may be a custodian taking time out from her day to ask a student in the hallway how her day is going. Your hero may be a retired banker turned substitute teacher who brings in leadership presentations for the classes he's teaching. Regardless of who your vision hero is, this hero can and will provide a tangible picture of the shared vision if you provide the platform for that to occur.

Ingraining a shared vision in the culture of your school will also require elaborate communication and celebration of the shared vision statement. We use the word *elaborate* here because when it seems like you've communicated and celebrated the vision enough, you need to do it again. If you're not careful, the constant barrage of demands and expectations on your teachers will send them in a million different directions, slowly steering them away from the shared vision without them even realizing it. Communicating and celebrating the shared vision will shine light on what is most important and will ensure that your staff see the value in their work and the value in the vision they were a part of creating.

Principals that effectively implement and sustain a shared vision in their school thoughtfully integrate their school's shared vision into the schedule of the school. For example, one principal conducts weekly staff huddles every Friday morning for fifteen minutes before school starts. This principal gathers staff together in a circle, or huddle, and reminds the staff of their shared vision, asks the staff what is helping to achieve the shared vision and what needs to be improved, and ends the huddle by celebrating specific stories from the week that highlight the shared vision in action. While staff huddles take time and effort, they provide a scheduled opportunity to help staff continue to move in the same direction. The following list contains other ways you can consistently communicate and celebrate the shared vision of your staff.

- **A drawing or poster:** Prepare high-quality color prints of your vision poster and post them in various locations so people can see and connect with them throughout the day.

- **Video:** Communicate how the vision becomes applicable in daily routines through video memos.

- **Audio:** It is important for people to hear your voice rather than someone else's when communicating the vision. Examples of stating the vision using an audio format include morning announcements, school podcasts, or audio files linked to staff newsletters.

- **Face-to-face meetings:** Face-to-face meetings are one of the best and most effective ways to communicate the vision. Examples include collaborative team meetings, school committees, and parent or teacher organization meetings.

- **Annual events:** Annual employee meetings such as back-to-school gatherings or end-of-the-year events are great for giving formal speeches related to the shared vision.

INSIGHTS FROM THE FIELD

"A good leader is able to communicate vision through actions, not just words. Observers will discover a leader's vision by seeing passion in action. A leader's vision matters because they are responsible for aiming the team's shared arrow toward the collective goal. A true leader doesn't demand followers; she inspires others to walk beside her and has a mindset of we over me."

—Special education strategist,
personal communication, August 11, 2020

Reflection

At the end of the chapter (page 132), you will find the "Developing a Shared Vision Rating Scale." The rating scale will help you assess your current state of developing and maintaining a shared vision, identify areas of strength and needs for improvement, and provide focus to your professional learning progress.

> ## What About the Support Staff?
>
> - Involve staff in the visioning process of the school. Ask them what they want the school to become.
>
> - Help staff see the reasons behind decisions. If they understand the reasons for doing something they are much more likely to buy into it. Giving real-life application is the key.
>
> - Empower staff to live and breathe the vision in all they do. Remind them they play an important role in modeling for students and staff the vision of the school.

Conclusion

This chapter focused on the question What matters most? by examining how to implement and sustain a shared vision in your school. Shared visions call for a unique combination of energy and empathy. As leaders, we put ourselves into the shoes of our teachers, seeking to understand their personal visions, so that we may align them with the visions of others among the staff. Then we use the shared vision as something to rally behind, constantly reminding our staff of our collectively desired destination that we can only get to when each and every person uses their unique talents, skills, and abilities to make the school great—something that it could not become without the individual contributions of all. A shared vision is not easy to create and is even harder to maintain. But, when we discover the personal visions within our schools, unite them into one shared vision, and take the vision beyond the crafting of a shared statement, we will help instill a direction for the school for years to come, establishing an enduring, lasting legacy.

Talk It Over: Reflection Guide for Discussions

Growing as a learner and leader takes thoughtful reflection. Interacting with this book's text and listening to the experiences of others will make you more fully aware of who you are as a leader and the steps you can take to grow. Thoughtful conversations take time and energy, but investing in each other through conversation will establish the support group you will need when the going gets tough.

1. **Introducing yourself to the topic:** What have been your experiences being a part of a group of people working toward one common purpose? What factors most influenced unifying the group?

2. **Looking inward:** When developing a shared vision, which leadership attributes or actions come most naturally to you? What have been your greatest challenges in developing a shared vision?

3. **Making connections:** Take a moment to interact with the following statement by highlighting, underlining, or writing in the margins. Jot down questions or connections that you have with the statement to your life, community, and world. Then, share out your thoughts.

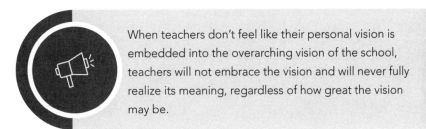

When teachers don't feel like their personal vision is embedded into the overarching vision of the school, teachers will not embrace the vision and will never fully realize its meaning, regardless of how great the vision may be.

4. **Applying it in practice:** Growing as a leader takes steps of action. You can do that with confidence when you share openly with others, supporting one another in those steps. Reflect on the "Developing a Shared Vision Rating Scale" (page 132). Where is your greatest need for growth? What step will you take to grow in that area?

Personal Vision Exercise

Directions: The goal of this exercise is to better understand your visions for the future of our school. Please respond to the following questions as thoroughly as possible. Then, using a large sheet of chart paper, prepare a visual representation of your personal vision to share with a small group.

1. What's going well for *you* in our school?

2. What could be improved for *you* in our school?

3. What does a perfect school look like, sound like, and feel like for *you*?

• What needs to be done now to make that happen for you and your students?

• What should be done in the future to make that happen for you and your students?

Reflection Questionnaire

Where Do We Go From Here?

1. What similarities in visions did you notice?

2. What differences in visions did you notice? Are these differences great enough that they should be addressed prior to moving forward?

3. What are the next steps to the visioning process that you would like to see?

4. Do you have any additional thoughts you'd like to share about our future shared vision at this time?

Developing a Shared Vision Rating Scale

Read each statement and reflect on how you rate in developing and maintaining a shared vision with your staff. Then, determine next steps for growth.

Discovering the Personal Visions Within Your School	Strongly Disagree	Somewhat Disagree	Somewhat Agree	Strongly Agree
I give my teachers time to reflect on their personal vision for the school.				
Next Steps:				
I know each of my teacher's personal visions for the school.				
Next Steps:				

Uniting Personal Visions Into One Shared Vision	Strongly Disagree	Somewhat Disagree	Somewhat Agree	Strongly Agree
I lead my staff in a process uniting personal visions into one shared vision.				
Next Steps:				
I provide opportunities for my staff to give feedback on the shared vision and will revisit the shared vision statement if necessary.				
Next Steps:				

Going Beyond the Crafting of a Shared Vision Statement	Strongly Disagree	Somewhat Disagree	Somewhat Agree	Strongly Agree
I model the behaviors and actions necessary to achieve the shared vision.				
Next Steps:				
I use vision heroes to help model the behaviors and actions necessary to achieve the shared vision.				
Next Steps:				
I communicate and celebrate the shared vision by building it into the school schedule.				
Next Steps:				

Conclusion

It's the last day of school on the last day of your career. You enter your office one final time with a question swirling in your mind: Where did the years go?

But soon your thoughts drift elsewhere, to the people you will leave behind. The people that you've served so tirelessly for so long. The people that make a difference in the lives of kids each and every day, your teachers. You hope that over the course of your career you have demonstrated the kind of leadership that gave each of your teachers a sense of purpose and belonging, helped them achieve more than they could have ever imagined, and provided the kind of support they so markedly deserved. But you have to ask yourself, "Did I do enough?"

The answer to that question may be a difficult one to find because the bottom line is, teaching is hard. So hard, in fact, that teachers are leaving a profession they love at a pace that is unsustainable. This has left our nation's state of education at a critical juncture: either find ways to keep our teachers in the profession or risk losing them for good, setting in motion devastating pedagogical, financial, and student learning consequences. Considering the high rates of dissatisfied, stressed, and burned-out teachers, it's clear that what we are currently doing *with*, *for*, and *to* our teachers is not working. It is also clear that you, the school leader, sit in the driver's seat, playing a critical role in the retention of your teachers. As the educational leader in your building, you hold the awesome responsibility to be the difference maker in the lives of your teachers, so that your teachers can make a difference in the lives of their students. In other words, unless we do something about teacher retention as leaders, we will continue to see teacher after teacher leave their callings in search of a place where they feel supported, a place where personal and professional growth is valued, and a place where their unique passions and differences are celebrated, honored, and considered an asset.

Throughout this book we've encouraged you to look at the retention factors within your control, knowing that who you are as a leader and the actions you do or do not take can have a dramatic impact on whether or not your teachers stay in your school. We've also encouraged you to consider that teacher retention is about helping teachers discover that who they are and what they do matter. When we keep our teachers in our schools, we have a chance to impact their lives for years to come, ultimately defining our legacy as their leader.

Lasting legacies do not come by chance, they come through thoughtful, deliberate steps you take as a leader. We've suggested these steps may resemble the nature of a stone hitting water. As you consciously take a step in your leadership, a ripple begins to form, influencing the lives of those around you. Eventually, that ripple moves outward, creating more ripples, and thus your impact on others expands. In this book we've asked you to consider this ripple effect through four legacy-building questions. Knowing the answers to these questions will broaden your lasting legacy and impact on those you are privileged to serve.

1. **Who am I?** The crux of your retention and legacy building efforts relies on your leadership authenticity. Authenticity *must* be the start of your leadership journey, as who you are as a person and a leader will make or break your leadership efforts. Leaders cannot fully develop teacher self-efficacy and collective staff efficacy, build trust, communicate effectively, or develop a shared vision without first knowing themselves.

2. **Who are you?** When you get to know yourself as an authentic leader, your attention can begin to turn outward, toward the teachers within your building. Leaving a lasting legacy and retaining your teachers require you to lead with a servant's heart, ultimately placing the needs of your teachers before your own. When you focus on who your teachers are, you can foster the necessary experiences and conditions that will instill beliefs and practices *within* your teachers, building their self-efficacy—the issue at the core of retention.

3. **Who are we?** As your teachers begin to believe in themselves, they in turn will have the capacity to look beyond themselves toward the collective school community. There is little doubt the profession of teaching and learning is too challenging and too complex to ever be considered a solitary endeavor. That is why schools are at their best when the individuals within them have a collective belief in their capabilities, relying on each other and being willing to share their unique strengths to benefit one another. When you make the development of your staff's collective efficacy a priority, you will eliminate a culture of fragmentation

and isolation in your school, promoting a culture of collaboration and interdependence.

4. **What matters most?** Knowing *who* to focus on in your legacy building efforts is vital, yet certain leadership practices will accelerate these efforts. Leaders with lasting legacies spend their time on building trusting relationships, listening with empathy, and developing a shared vision throughout their school. They do this because they know the beliefs, actions, and interactions of their staff hinge on the modeling they provide as the leader. Great leaders focus on the things that matter most by keeping both people *and* results in mind. They know results will come when they focus on supporting their followers, helping them feel trusted, valued, heard, and part of something bigger than themselves.

Either sometime soon, a long time from now, or somewhere in between, the last day of school on the last day of your career will come. Whenever that day does come, you will reflect on your time as a leader and eventually ask yourself the question, "Did I do enough for those I served?" Most of us answer this question incrementally, little by little, as we hear stories about our leadership and the things we did that meant the most to our followers. For some of us, the answer will come quickly, as we attend an event in our honor. Regardless of when or how you find the answer to that question, what do you think your teachers will say? Will they talk about your authenticity and how you stayed true to your values no matter what? Will they comment on your ability to unite a group of people under one common cause, helping them believe in the power of themselves and each other? Will they speak of the way you always made them feel heard and trusted? The irony of school leadership is that your legacy will not live on through the programs, policies, or procedures you put in place throughout your tenure, but it will live on within and through the people you lead. At the beginning of this book, we defined a school leader's legacy as:

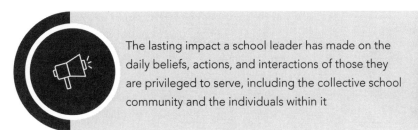

The lasting impact a school leader has made on the daily beliefs, actions, and interactions of those they are privileged to serve, including the collective school community and the individuals within it

We leave you now with "The Difference Maker's Creed" (page 138), a reminder of the primary aims that will guide your path toward making a lasting difference in your teachers' lives. Our hope and desire for you are that you will use this creed along with the thoughts and tools provided in this book, walk alongside your teachers, and start the ripple of your leadership legacy today.

The Difference Maker's Creed

I am a difference maker.
I lead with # Authenticity

knowing who I am as a person and leader is more important than
my title, accolades, or personal achievements.

I am a difference maker.
I develop # Self-Efficacy

in my teachers knowing their belief in themselves and their
capabilities will empower them to face all that lies before them.

I am a difference maker.
I build # Collective Efficacy

in my staff knowing their belief in each other will take them
further than they could ever imagine going alone.

I am a difference maker.
I value # Trust

as an integral part of success in my school, knowing
positive relationships are the key to our school's culture.

I am a difference maker.
I listen with # Empathy

to my teachers knowing I will never fully understand where they are
coming from yet caring enough for them to try to understand anyway.

I am a difference maker.
I unite a shared # Vision

with my staff knowing the collection of our unique differences and
strengths is the only thing that will get us to where we want to go.

I am a difference maker.
I forge my # Legacy

through the daily beliefs, actions, and interactions
of those I am privileged to serve.

For I am a difference maker.

References and Resources

Afzal, S., Arshad, M., Saleem, S., & Farooq, O. (2019). The impact of perceived supervisor support on employees' turnover intention and task performance. *Journal of Management Development, 38*(5), 369–382.

Ainsworth, L. (2013). *Prioritizing the Common Core: Identifying specific standards to emphasize the most*. Englewood, CO: Lead + Learn Press.

Aldridge, J. M., & Fraser, B. J. (2016). Teachers' views of their school climate and its relationship with teacher self-efficacy and job satisfaction. *Learning Environments Research, 19*(2), 291–307.

Allensworth, E., Ponisciak, S., & Mazzeo, C. (2009). *The schools teachers leave: Teacher mobility in Chicago public schools*. Accessed at https://files.eric.ed.gov/fulltext/ED505882.pdf on March 2, 2021.

Althauser, K. (2015). Job-embedded professional development: Its impact on teacher self-efficacy and student performance. *Teacher Development, 19*(2), 210–225.

American Federation of Teachers. (2017). *2017 educator quality of work life survey*. Washington, DC: Author. Accessed at www.aft.org/sites/default/files/2017_eqwl_survey_web.pdf on March 2, 2021.

Angelle, P., & Teague, G. M. (2014). Teacher leadership and collective efficacy: Teacher perceptions in three US school districts. *Journal of Educational Administration, 52*(6), 738–753.

Avanzi, L., Schuh, S. C., Fraccaroli, F., & van Dick, R. (2015). Why does organizational identification relate to reduced employee burnout? The mediating influence of social support and collective efficacy. *Work and Stress, 29*(1), 1–10.

Avolio, B. J., Gardner, W. L., Walumbwa, F. O., Luthans, F., & May, D. R. (2004). Unlocking the mask: A look at the process by which authentic leaders impact follower attitudes and behaviors. *The Leadership Quarterly, 15*(6), 801–823.

Bandura, A. (1993). Perceived self-efficacy in cognitive development and functioning. *Educational Psychologist, 28*(2), 117–148.

Bandura, A. (1994). Self-efficacy. In V. S. Ramachaudran (Ed.), *Encyclopedia of human behavior* (Vol. 4, pp. 71–81). New York: Academic Press.

Bandura, A. (1998). Personal and collective efficacy in human adaptation and change. In J. G. Adair, D. Belanger, & K. L. Dion (Eds.), *Advances in psychological science, vol. 1.* (pp. 51–71). Hove, England: Psychology Press.

Bandura, A. (2000). Exercise of human agency through collective efficacy. *Current Directions in Psychological Science, 9*(3), 75–78.

Bandura, A. (2006). Guide for constructing self-efficacy scales. In F. Pajares & T. Urdan (Eds.), *Self-efficacy beliefs of adolescents* (Vol. 5, pp. 307–337). Greenwich, CT: Information Age.

Bird, J. J., Wang, C., Watson, J., & Murray, L. (2012). Teacher and principal perceptions of authentic leadership: Implications for trust, engagement, and intention to return. *Journal of School Leadership, 22*(3), 425–461.

Bjork, E. L., & Bjork, R. A. (2011). Making things hard on yourself, but in a good way: Creating desirable difficulties to enhance learning. In M. A. Gernsbacher and J. Pomerantz (Eds.), *Psychology and the real world: Essays illustrating fundamental contributions to society* (2nd ed., pp. 59–68). New York: Worth.

Bodie, G. D. (2011). The active-empathic listening scale (AELS): Conceptualization and evidence of validity within the interpersonal domain. *Communication Quarterly, 59*(3), 277–295.

Bondie, R., & Dockterman, D. (2018). *What strategy is most useful in promoting self-efficacy in educators and in learners?* Accessed at https://researchmap.digitalpromise.org/ask_a_researcher /strategy-useful-promoting-self-efficacy-educators-learners/ on March 2, 2021.

Bolman, L. G., & Deal, T. E. (2013). *Reframing organizations: Artistry, choice, and leadership.* San Francisco: Jossey-Bass.

Boske, C., Osanloo, A., & Newcomb, W. S. (2017). Exploring empathy to promote social justice leadership in schools. *Journal of School Leadership, 27*(3), 361–391.

BrainyQuote. (n.d.). *Mahatma Gandhi quotes.* Accessed atwww.brainyquote.com/quotes/mahatma _gandhi_150726 on March 3, 2021.

Brouwer, P., Brekelmans, M., Nieuwenhuis, A. F. M., & Simons, R. J. (2012). Communities of practice in the school workplace. *Journal of Educational Administration, 50*(3), 346–364.

Burkhauser, S. (2017). How much do school principals matter when it comes to teacher working conditions? *Educational Evaluation and Policy Analysis, 39*(1), 126–145.

Camara, M., Bacigalupe, G., & Padilla, P. (2017). The role of social support in adolescents: Are you helping me or stressing me out? *International Journal of Adolescence and Youth, 22*(2), 123–136.

Carver-Thomas, D., & Darling-Hammond, L. (2017). *Teacher turnover: Why it matters and what we can do about it.* Palo Alto, CA: Learning Policy Institute. Accessed at https:// learningpolicyinstitute.org/sites/default/files/product-files/Teacher_Turnover_REPORT.pdf on March 2, 2021.

Cashman, K. (2018). *Leadership from the inside out: Becoming a leader for life.* Portland: Ringgold.

Center on the Developing Child. (2021). *ACEs and toxic stress: Frequently asked questions.* Accessed at https://developingchild.harvard.edu/resources/aces-and-toxic-stress-frequently-asked-questions/ on July 15, 2021.

Chai, D. S., Hwang, S. J., & Joo, B. K. (2017). Transformational leadership and organizational commitment in teams: The mediating roles of shared vision and team-goal commitment. *Performance Improvement Quarterly, 30*(2), 137–158.

Clement, M. (2017). Why combatting teachers' stress is everyone's job. *The Clearing House: A Journal of Educational Strategies, Issues, and Ideas, 90*(4), 135–138.

Covey, S. R. (2004). *The 7 habits of highly effective people: Powerful lessons in personal change.* New York: Simon & Schuster.

Croft, A., Coggshall, J. G., Dolan, M., & Powers, E. (2010). *Job-embedded professional development: What it is, who is responsible, and how to get it done well.* Accessed at https://files.eric.ed.gov/full text/ED520830.pdf on March 2, 2021.

Dahlkamp, S., Peters, M. L., & Schumacher, G. (2017). Principal self-efficacy, school climate, and teacher retention: A multi-level analysis. *Alberta Journal of Educational Research, 63*(4), 357–376.

Darling-Hammond, L., Hyler, M. E., & Gardner, M. (2017). *Effective teacher professional development.* Palo Alto, CA: Learning Policy Institute. Accessed at https://learningpolicyinstitute .org/sites/default/files/product-files/Effective_Teacher_Professional_Development_REPORT.pdf on March 2, 2021.

Deci, E. L., Olafsen, A. H., & Ryan, R. M. (2017). Self-determination theory in work organizations: The state of a science. *Annual Review of Organizational Psychology and Organizational Behavior, 4*, 19–43.

de Heus, P., & Diekstra, R. F. W. (1999). Do teachers burn out more easily? A comparison of teachers with other social professions on work stress and burnout symptoms. In R. Vandenberghe & A. M. Huberman (Eds.), *Understanding and preventing teacher burnout: A sourcebook of international research and practice* (pp. 269–284). Cambridge, England: Cambridge University Press.

Demaray, M. K., Malecki, C. K., Secord, S. M., & Lyell, K. M. (2012). Promoting social support. In S. E. Brock & S. R. Jimerson (Eds.), *Best practices in crisis prevention and intervention in the schools* (2nd ed., pp. 79–95). Bethesda, MD: National Association of School Psychologists.

Demir, S. (2020). The role of self-efficacy in job satisfaction, organizational commitment, motivation, and job involvement. *Eurasian Journal of Educational Research, 20*(85), 205–224.

DePree, M. (2004). *Leadership is an art.* New York: Currency Doubleday.

Derrington, M. L., & Angelle, P. S. (2013). Teacher leadership and collective efficacy: Connections and links. *International Journal of Teacher Leadership, 4*(1), 1–13.

DeWitt, P. M. (2018). *School climate: Leading with collective efficacy.* Thousand Oaks, CA: Corwin Press.

Dias-Lacy, S. L., & Guirguis, R. V. (2017). Challenges for new teachers and ways of coping with them. *Journal of Education and Learning, 6*(3), 265–272.

Donohoo, J. (2018). Collective teacher efficacy research: Productive patterns of behaviour and other positive consequences. *Journal of Educational Change, 19*(3), 323–345.

Donohoo, J., Hattie, J., & Eells, R. (2018). The power of collective efficacy. *Educational Leadership, 75*(6), 40–44.

Dowden, A. R., Warren, J. M., & Kambui, H. (2014). *Three tiered model toward improved self-awareness and self-care.* Accessed at www.counseling.org/docs/default-source/vistas/article_30.pdf on March 2, 2021.

DuFour, R. (2015). *In praise of American educators: And how they can become even better.* Bloomington, IN: Solution Tree Press.

DuFour, R., DuFour, R., Eaker, R., Many, T. W., & Mattos, M. (2016). *Learning by doing: A handbook for Professional Learning Communities at Work* (3rd ed.). Bloomington, IN: Solution Tree Press.

Duncan, P., Green, M., Gergen, E., & Ecung, W. (2017). Authentic leadership—is it more than emotional intelligence? *Administrative Issues Journal, 7*(2), 11–22.

Educators for Excellence. (2020). *Voices from the classroom: A survey of America's educators.* Accessed at https://e4e.org/sites/default/files/voices_from_the_classroom_2020.pdf on March 2, 2021.

Erdem, M., İlğan, A., & Uçar, H. İ. (2014). Relationship between learning organization and job satisfaction of primary school teachers. *International Online Journal of Educational Sciences, 6*(1), 8–20.

Eurich, T. (2018). *What self-awareness really is (and how to cultivate it).* Accessed at https://hbr.org/2018/01/what-self-awareness-really-is-and-how-to-cultivate-it on March 2, 2021.

Eva, N., Robin, M., Sendjaya, S., van Dierendonck, D., & Liden, R. C. (2019). Servant leadership: A systematic review and call for future research. *The Leadership Quarterly, 30*(1), 111–132.

Feng, F. (2016). School principals' authentic leadership and teachers' psychological capital: Teachers' perspectives. *International Education Studies, 9*(10), 245–255.

Fullan, M. (2014). *The principal: Three keys to maximizing impact.* San Francisco: Jossey-Bass.

Gallup. (2014). *State of America's schools: The path to winning again in education.* Washington, DC: Author.

George, B. (2007). *True north: Discover your authentic leadership.* San Francisco: Jossey-Bass.

George, B. (2015). *Discover your true north.* Hoboken, NJ: Wiley.

Goldrick, L. (2016). *Support from the start: A 50-state review of policies on new educator induction and mentoring.* Accessed at https://newteachercenter.org/wp-content/uploads/2016CompleteReport StatePolicies.pdf on March 2, 2021.

Gordon, J., & Smith, M. (2015). *You win in the locker room first: The 7 C's to build a winning team in business, sports, and life.* Hoboken, NJ: Wiley.

Greenleaf, R. K. (1970). *The servant as leader.* Atlanta, GA: Robert K. Greenleaf Center for Servant Leadership.

Gurin, P., Nagda, B. A., & Zúñiga, X. (2013). *Dialogue across difference: Practice, theory, and research on intergroup dialogue.* New York: Russell Sage Foundation.

Hall, M. (2014). *Thrive: Digging deep, reaching out.* Grand Rapids, MI: Zondervan.

Handford, V., & Leithwood, K. (2013). Why teachers trust school leaders. *Journal of Educational Administration, 51*(2), 194–212.

Hattie, J. (2012). *Visible learning for teachers: Maximizing impact on learning.* London: Routledge.

Hattie, J., & Yates, G. C. R. (2014). *Visible learning and the science of how we learn.* London: Routledge.

Haydon, T., Leko, M. M., & Stevens, D. (2018). Teacher stress: Sources, effects, and protective factors. *Journal of Special Education Leadership, 31*(2), 99–107.

Haynes, M. (2014). *On the path to equity: Improving the effectiveness of beginning teachers.* Washington, DC: Alliance for Excellent Education.

Hirst, G., Walumbwa, F., Aryee, S., Butarbutar, I., & Chen, C. J. H. (2016). A multi-level investigation of authentic leadership as an antecedent of helping behavior. *Journal of Business Ethics, 139*(3), 485–499.

Hoy, W. K. (1990). Organizational climate and culture: A conceptual analysis of the school workplace. *Journal of Educational and Psychological Consultation, 1*(2), 149–168.

Hoy, W. K., Tarter, C. J., & Hoy, A. W. (2006). Academic optimism of schools: A force for student achievement. *American Educational Research Journal, 43*(3), 425–446.

Hughes, A. L., Matt, J. J., & O'Reilly, F. L. (2015). Principal support is imperative to the retention of teachers in hard-to-staff schools. *Journal of Education and Training Studies, 3*(1), 129–134.

Ingersoll, R., & May, H. (2012). The magnitude, destinations, and determinants of mathematics and science teacher turnover. *Educational Evaluation and Policy Analysis, 34*(4), 435–464.

Ingersoll, R., & May, H. (2016). *Minority teacher recruitment, employment, and retention: 1987 to 2013* (Research brief). Palo Alto, CA: Learning Policy Institute.

Ingersoll, R., May, H., & Collins, G. (2017). *Minority teacher recruitment, employment, and retention: 1987 to 2013.* Palo Alto, CA: Learning Policy Institute.

Ingersoll, R., May, H., & Collins, G. (2019). Recruitment, employment, retention and the minority teacher shortage. *Education Policy Analysis Archives, 27*(37), 2–42.

Ingersoll, R., Merrill, L., & May, H. (2016). Do accountability policies push teachers out? *Educational Leadership, 73*(8), 44–49.

Ingersoll, R., Merrill, L., & Stuckey, D. (2014). *Seven trends: The transformation of the teaching force.* Philadelphia, PA: Consortium for Policy Research in Education.

Ingersoll, R., & Strong, M. (2011). The impact of induction and mentoring programs for beginning teachers: A critical review of the research. *Review of Educational Research, 81*(2), 201–233.

Jackson, E. (2014, May 11). *The top 8 reasons your best people are about to quit—and how you can keep them.* Accessed at www.forbes.com/sites/ericjackson/2014/05/11/the-top-8-reasons-your-best-people-are-about-to-quit-and-how-you-can-keep-them/#24808c365c45 on March 3, 2021.

Johnson, S. M., Kraft, M. A., & Papay, J. P. (2012). How context matters in high-need schools: The effects of teachers' working conditions on their professional satisfaction and their students' achievement. *Teachers College Record, 114*(10), 1–39.

Kanaslan, E. K., & Iyem, C. (2016). Is 360 degree feedback appraisal an effective way of performance evaluation? *International Journal of Academic Research in Business and Social Sciences, 6*(5), 172–182.

Kanold, T. D. (2011). *The five disciplines of PLC leaders.* Bloomington, IN: Solution Tree Press.

Keyes, T. S. (2019). A qualitative inquiry: Factors that promote classroom belonging and engagement among high school students. *School Community Journal, 29*(1), 171–200.

Kimble, P., & Bamford-Wade, A. (2013). The journey of discovering compassionate listening. *Journal of Holistic Nursing, 31*(4), 285–290.

Knight, J., Elford, M., Hock, M., Dunekack, D., Bradley, B., Deshler, D. D., & Knight, D. (2015). 3 steps to great coaching: A simple but powerful instructional coaching cycle nets results. *Journal of Staff Development, 36*(1), 10–18.

Kouzes, J. M., & Posner, B. (2009). To lead, create a shared vision. *Harvard Business Review*, *87*(1), 20–21.

Kutsyuruba, B., & Walker, K. (2015). The role of trust in developing teacher leaders through early-career induction and mentoring programs. *Antistasis*, *5*(1), 32–36.

Ladd, H. F. (2011). Teachers' perceptions of their working conditions: How predictive of planned and actual teacher movement? *Educational Evaluation and Policy Analysis*, *33*(2), 235–261.

Lai, F. T., Li, E. P., Ji, M., Wong, W. W., & Lo, S. K. (2016). What are the inclusive teaching tasks that require the highest self-efficacy? *Teaching and Teacher Education*, *59*, 338–346.

Lambersky, J. (2016). Understanding the human side of school leadership: Principals' impact on teachers' morale, self-efficacy, stress, and commitment. *Leadership and Policy in Schools*, *15*(4), 379–405.

Lander, J. (2018, October 7). *Secondary traumatic stress for educators: Understanding and mitigating the effects*. Accessed at www.kqed.org/mindshift/52281/secondary-traumatic-stress-for-educators -understanding-and-mitigating-the-effects on March 3, 2021.

Levin, S., & Bradley, K. (2019). *Understanding and addressing principal turnover: A review of the research*. Reston, VA: National Association of Secondary School Principals.

Liu, L., Gou, Z., & Zuo, J. (2016). Social support mediates loneliness and depression in elderly people. *Journal of Health Psychology*, *21*(5), 750–758.

Liu, S., & Hallinger, P. (2018). Principal instructional leadership, teacher self-efficacy, and teacher professional learning in China: Testing a mediated-effects model. *Educational Administration Quarterly*, *54*(4), 501–528.

Liu, Y., & Liao, W. (2019). Professional development and teacher efficacy: Evidence from the 2013 TALIS. *School Effectiveness and School Improvement*, *30*(4), 487–509.

Loughland T., & Ryan, M. (2020). Beyond the measures: The antecedents of teacher collective efficacy in professional learning. *Professional Development in Education*, 1–10.

Mack, J. C., Johnson, A., Jones-Rincon, A., Tsatenawa, V., & Howard, K. (2019). Why do teachers leave? A comprehensive occupational health study evaluating intent-to-quit in public school teachers. *Journal of Applied Biobehavioral Research*, *24*(1), e12160.

Martin, T. L., & Rains, C. L. (2018). *Stronger together: Answering the questions of collaborative leadership*. Bloomington, IN: Solution Tree Press.

Marzano, R. J., Warrick, P. B., Rains, C. L., & DuFour, R. (2018). *Leading a high reliability school*. Bloomington, IN: Solution Tree Press.

Maslach, C., & Leiter, M. P. (2016). Understanding the burnout experience: Recent research and its implications for psychiatry. *World Psychiatry*, *15*(2), 103–111.

Maxwell, J. (2005). *Developing the leader within you*. Nashville, TN: Thomas Nelson Publishers.

McRae, C., & Nainby, K. (2015). Engagement beyond interruption: A performative perspective on listening and ethics. *Educational Studies*, *51*(2), 168–184.

Miao, C., Humphrey, R. H., & Qian, S. (2018). Emotional intelligence and authentic leadership: A meta-analysis. *Leadership and Organization Development Journal*, *39*(5), 679–690.

Nagda, B. A. (2019). Intergroup dialogue: Engaging difference for social change leadership development. *New Directions for Student Leadership*, 29–46.

National Child Traumatic Stress Network. (n.d.). *Secondary traumatic stress.* Accessed at www.nctsn .org/trauma-informed-care/secondary-traumatic-stress on March 3, 2021.

Okubanjo, A. O. (2014). Organizational commitment and job satisfaction as determinant of primary school teachers' turnover intention. *Higher Education of Social Science, 7*(1), 173–179.

Palmer, P. J. (1998). Leading from within. In L. C. Spears (Ed.), *Insights on leadership: Service, stewardship, spirit, and servant-leadership* (pp. 197–208). New York: Wiley.

Perera-Diltz, D. M. (2017). Listening, empathic. In J. Carlson & S. B. Dermer (Eds.), *The SAGE encyclopedia of marriage, family, and couples counseling* (Vol. 3, pp. 966–969). Thousand Oaks, CA: SAGE.

Phillips, O. (2015, March 30). *Revolving door of teachers costs schools billions every year.* Accessed at www.npr.org/sections/ed/2015/03/30/395322012/the-hidden-costs-of-teacher-turnover on March 3, 2021.

Podolsky, A., Kini, T., Bishop, J., & Darling-Hammond, L. (2016). *Solving the teacher shortage: How to attract and retain excellent educators.* Palo Alto, CA: Learning Policy Institute. Accessed at https://files.eric.ed.gov/fulltext/ED606767.pdf on March 3, 2021.

Reeves, D. B. (2010). *Transforming professional development into student results.* Alexandria, VA: Association for Supervision and Curriculum Development.

Rego, A., Sousa, F., Marques, C., & e Cunha, M. P. (2012). Authentic leadership promoting employees' psychological capital and creativity. *Journal of Business Research, 65*(3), 429–437.

Ribeiro, N., Duarte, A. P., & Filipe, R. (2018). How authentic leadership promotes individual performance: Mediating role of organizational citizenship behavior and creativity. *International Journal of Productivity and Performance Management, 67*(9), 1585–1607.

Samuels, C. A., & Harwin, A. (2018, December 4). *Shortage of special educators adds to classroom pressures.* Accessed at www.edweek.org/leadership/shortage-of-special-educators-adds-to-classroom -pressures/2018/12 on June 11, 2021.

Saylor, C. F., & Leach, J. B. (2009). Perceived bullying and social support in students accessing special inclusion programming. *Journal of Developmental and Physical Disabilities, 21*(1), 69–80.

Sergiovanni, T. J., & Green, R. L. (2015). *The principalship: A reflective practice perspective* (7th ed.). Boston: Pearson.

Shahidi, N., Shamsnia, S. A., & Baezat, S. (2015). Studying the relationship between self-efficacy and organizational citizenship behavior (Case study: Islamic Azad University–Zone 1). *International Research Journal of Applied and Basic Sciences, 9*(9), 1499–1503.

Shaw, J., & Newton, J. (2014). Teacher retention and satisfaction with a servant leader as principal. *Education, 135*(1), 101–106.

Shernoff, E. S., Mehta, T. G., Atkins, M. S., Torf, R., & Spencer, J. (2011). A qualitative study of the sources and impact of stress among urban teachers. *School Mental Health, 3*(2), 59–69.

Simon, N. S., & Johnson, S. M. (2015). Teacher turnover in high-poverty schools: What we know and can do. *Teachers College Record, 117*(3), 1–36.

Sinek, S. (2014). *Leaders eat last: Why some teams pull together and others don't.* New York: Portfolio/Penguin.

Skaalvik, E. M., & Skaalvik, S. (2016). Teacher stress and teacher self-efficacy as predictors of engagement, emotional exhaustion, and motivation to leave the teaching profession. *Creative Education, 7*(13), 1785–1799.

Smetackovaa, I. (2017). Self-efficacy and burnout syndrome among teachers. *The European Journal of Social and Behavioural Sciences, 20*(3), 2476–2488.

Stavros, J. M., Godwin, L. N., & Cooperrider, D. L. (2016). Appreciative inquiry: Organization development and the strengths revolution. In W. J. Rothwell, J. M. Stavros, & R. L. Sullivan (Eds.), *Practicing organization development: Leading transformation and change* (4th ed., pp. 96–116). Hoboken, NJ: Wiley.

Stoner, J. L. (n.d.). *How to create a shared vision that works.* Accessed at https://seapointcenter.com/how-to-create-a-shared-vision/ on March 3, 2021.

Storring, K. (2016). *Walk with me: The first step is engaging at a human level with a compassionate, listening ear.* Accessed at www.alternativesjournal.ca/walk-me on March 3, 2021.

Sutcher, L., Darling-Hammond, L., & Carver-Thomas, D. (2016). *A coming crisis in teaching? Teacher supply, demand, and shortages in the U.S.* Palo Alto, CA: Learning Policy Institute. Accessed at https://learningpolicyinstitute.org/sites/default/files/product-files/A_Coming_Crisis_in_Teaching_REPORT.pdf on March 3, 2021.

Thapa, A., Cohen, J., Guffey, S., & Higgins-D'Alessandro, A. (2013). A review of school climate research. *Review of Educational Research, 83*(3), 357–385.

Thiers, N. (2016). Educators deserve better: A conversation with Richard DuFour. *Educational Leadership, 73*(8), 10–16.

Torres, A. C. (2016). The uncertainty of high expectations: How principals influence relational trust and teacher turnover in no excuses charter schools. *Journal of School Leadership, 26*(1), 61–91.

Totaro, S., & Wise, M. (2018). New teacher immersion. *Educational Leadership, 75*(8), 12–17.

Tschannen-Moran, M. (2014). *Trust matters: Leadership for successful schools* (2nd ed.). San Francisco: Jossey-Bass.

Tschannen-Moran, M., & Gareis, C. R. (2015). Faculty trust in the principal: An essential ingredient in high-performing schools. *Journal of Educational Administration, 53*(1), 66–92.

Turkmen, F., & Gul, I. (2017). The effects of secondary school administrators' servant leadership behaviors on teachers' organizational commitment. *Journal of Education and Training Studies, 5*(12), 110–119.

van Niekerk, M., & Botha, J. (2017). Value-based leadership approach: A way for principals to revive the value of values in schools. *Educational Research and Reviews, 12*(3), 133–142.

Viinamäki, O. P. (2012). Why leaders fail in introducing values-based leadership? An elaboration of feasible steps, challenges, and suggestions for practitioners. *International Journal of Business and Management, 7*(9), 28–39.

Visible Learning. (2021). *Collective teacher efficacy (CTE) according to John Hattie.* Accessed at visible-learning.org/2018/03/collective-teacher-efficacy-hattie/ on June 13, 2021.

Waks, L. J. (Ed.). (2015). *Listening to teach: Beyond didactic pedagogy.* Albany, NY: SUNY Press.

Walumbwa, F. O., Avolio, B. J., Gardner, W. L., Wernsing, T. S., & Peterson, S. J. (2008). Authentic leadership: Development and validation of a theory-based measure. *Journal of Management, 34*(1), 89–126.

Wang, Y. D. (2014). Building trust in E-learning. *Athens Journal of Education, 1*(1), 9–18.

Warner-Griffin, C., Cunningham, B. C., & Noel, A. (2018). *Public school teacher autonomy, satisfaction, job security, and commitment: 1999–2000 and 2011–12.* Accessed at https://nces .ed.gov/pubs2018/2018103.pdf on March 3, 2021.

Weibenfels, M., Benick, M., & Perels, F. (2021). Can teacher self-efficacy act as a buffer against burnout in inclusive classrooms? *Journal of Educational Research, 109,* 1–12.

Weiss, M., Razinskas, S., Backmann, J., & Hoegl, M. (2018). Authentic leadership and leaders' mental well-being: An experience sampling study. *Leadership Quarterly, 29*(2), 309–321.

Worth, J., & Van den Brande, J. (2019). *Teacher labour market in England: Annual report 2019.* Accessed at https://files.eric.ed.gov/fulltext/ED594396.pdf on March 3, 2021.

Index

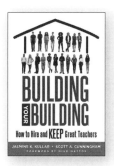

Building Your Building
Jasmine K. Kullar and Scott A. Cunningham
A growing teacher attrition rate, combined with fewer teachers entering the profession, has created a teacher shortage in many schools. In *Building Your Building*, the authors detail how school administrators can overcome these challenges to ensure they hire—and retain—great teachers.
BKF896

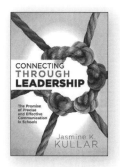

Connecting Through Leadership
Jasmine K. Kullar
The success of a school greatly depends on the ability of its leaders to communicate effectively. Rely on *Connecting Through Leadership* to help you strengthen your communication skills to inspire, motivate, and connect with every member of your school community.
BKF927

The Deliberate and Courageous Principal
Rhonda J. Roos
Fully step into your power as a school principal. By diving deep into five essential leadership actions and five essential leadership skills, you will learn how to grow in your role and accomplish incredible outcomes for your students and staff.
BKG013

Responding to Resistance
William A. Sommers
Educational leadership is never conflict free. In *Responding to Resistance*, author William A. Sommers acknowledges this reality and presents school leaders with wide-ranging strategies to decisively address conflict involving staff, students, parents, and other key stakeholders.
BKF955

Solution Tree | Press

Visit SolutionTree.com or call 800.733.6786 to order.

Wait! Your professional development journey doesn't have to end with the last pages of this book.

We realize improving student learning doesn't happen overnight. And your school or district shouldn't be left to puzzle out all the details of this process alone.

No matter where you are on the journey, we're committed to helping you get to the next stage.

Take advantage of everything from **custom workshops** to **keynote presentations** and **interactive web and video conferencing**. We can even help you develop an action plan tailored to fit your specific needs.

Let's get the conversation started.

Call 888.763.9045 today.

SolutionTree.com